Contents

W9-ANI-052

ADDISON WESLEY

Math
Makes Sense

6

Practice and Homework Book

Authors

Peggy Morrow   Maggie Martin Connell

PEARSON

Education
Canada

Elementary Math Team Leader
Diane Wyman

Publisher
Claire Burnett

Product Manager
Kathleen Crosbie

Publishing Team
Lesley Haynes
Enid Haley
Ellen Davidson
Marg Bukta
Lynne Gulliver
Stephanie Cox
Kaari Turk
Judy Wilson

Design
Word & Image Design Studio Inc.

Typesetting
ArtPlus Design and Communications

ISBN 0-321-24227-0

Printed and bound in Canada.

3 4 5 -- WC -- 10 09 08

To the Teacher

This Practice and Homework Book provides reinforcement of the concepts and skills explored in the *Addison Wesley Math Makes Sense 6* program.

There are two sections in the book. The first section follows the sequence of *Math Makes Sense 6 Student Book*. It is intended for use throughout the year as you teach the program. A two-page spread supports the content of each core lesson in the Student Book.

In each Lesson:

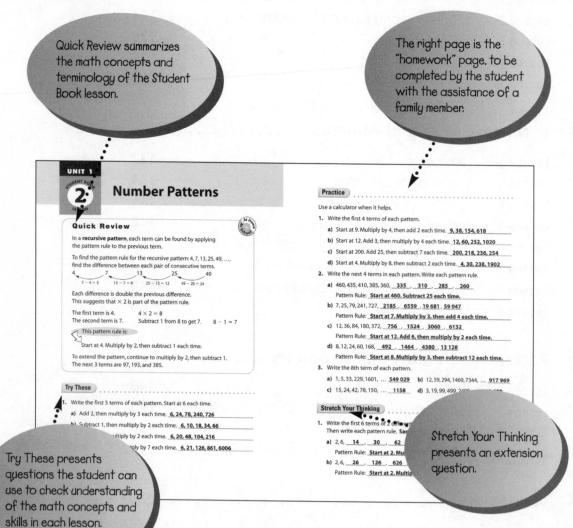

Quick Review summarizes the math concepts and terminology of the Student Book lesson.

The right page is the "homework" page, to be completed by the student with the assistance of a family member.

Try These presents questions the student can use to check understanding of the math concepts and skills in each lesson.

Stretch Your Thinking presents an extension question.

Math at Home

The second section of the book, on pages 165 to 176, consists of 3 pull-out **Math at Home** magazines. These fun pages contain intriguing activities, puzzles, rhymes, and games to encourage home involvement. The perforated design lets you remove, fold, and send home this eight-page magazine after the student has completed Units 3, 7, and 11.

To the Family

This book will help your child practise the math concepts and skills that have been explored in the classroom. As you assist your child to complete each page, you have an opportunity to become involved in your child's mathematical learning.

The left page of each lesson contains a summary of the main concepts and terminology of the lesson. Use this page with your child to review the work done in class. The right page contains practice.

Here are some ways you can help:

- With your child, read over the Quick Review. Encourage your child to talk about the content and explain it to you in his or her own words.
- Read the instructions with (or for) your child to ensure your child understands what to do.
- Encourage your child to explain his or her thinking.
- Some of the pages require specific materials. You may wish to gather items such as a centimetre ruler, index cards, a measuring tape, scissors, cubes numbered from 1 to 6, and paper clips.

Many of the Practice sections contain games that will also improve your child's math skills. You may have other ideas for activities your child can share with the rest of the class.

The **Math at Home** pull-out pages 165 to 176 provide more fun activities.

Input/Output Machines

Quick Review

At Home
At School

This Input/Output machine divides each input number by 2, then adds 3.

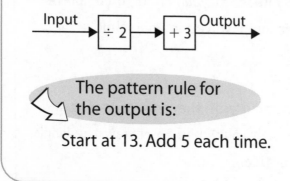

Input → ÷ 2 → + 3 → Output

The pattern rule for the output is:

Start at 13. Add 5 each time.

Input	Output
20	13
30	18
40	23
50	28

Output rule
> add 5

Try These

Complete the table for each Input/Output machine.
Write the pattern rule for each output.

1. Input → ÷ 2 → + 7 → Output

Input	Output
20	
18	
16	
14	

2. Input → × 4 → − 1 → Output

Input	Output
12	
13	
14	
15	

_____

_____

_____

_____

1. Complete the table for each Input/Output machine.
   Write the pattern rule for each output.

a) Input → $+ 5$ → $\times 4$ Output →

Input	Output
9	
10	
11	
12	

_____

_____

b) Input → $\times 7$ → $- 3$ Output →

Input	Output
6	
7	
8	
9	

_____

_____

2. The table shows the input and output from
   a machine with two operations.

   a) Write the numbers and the operations
      used by the Input/Output machine.

      _____

   b) Write the next 3 input and output numbers.

      _____

Input	Output
25	15
30	18
35	21
40	24

Stretch Your Thinking . . . .

The first 5 input numbers for a machine
are 2527, 2577, 2627, 2677, and 2727.
The first 5 output numbers for the machine
are 5061, 5161, 5261, 5361, and 5461.
Record the numbers and the operations in the machine.

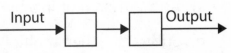

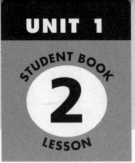

Number Patterns

UNIT 1

STUDENT BOOK

2

LESSON

At Home
At School

Quick Review

In a **recursive pattern**, each term can be found by applying the pattern rule to the previous term.

To find the pattern rule for the recursive pattern: 4, 7, 13, 25, 49, …, find the difference between each pair of consecutive terms.

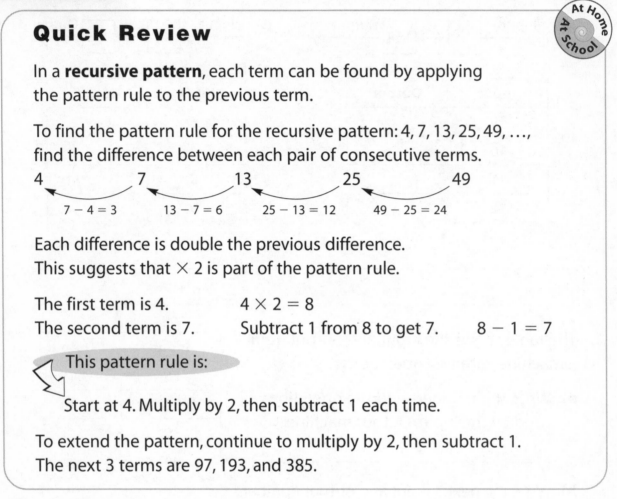

4   7   13   25   49

7 − 4 = 3   13 − 7 = 6   25 − 13 = 12   49 − 25 = 24

Each difference is double the previous difference.
This suggests that × 2 is part of the pattern rule.

The first term is 4.   4 × 2 = 8
The second term is 7.   Subtract 1 from 8 to get 7.   8 − 1 = 7

This pattern rule is:

Start at 4. Multiply by 2, then subtract 1 each time.

To extend the pattern, continue to multiply by 2, then subtract 1.
The next 3 terms are 97, 193, and 385.

Try These . . . .

1. Write the first 5 terms of each pattern. Start at 6 each time.

   a) Add 2, then multiply by 3 each time. _____

   b) Subtract 1, then multiply by 2 each time. _____

   c) Add 4, then multiply by 2 each time. _____

   d) Subtract 3, then multiply by 7 each time. _____

4

Use a calculator when it helps.

1. Write the first 4 terms of each pattern.

   a) Start at 9. Multiply by 4, then add 2 each time. _____

   b) Start at 12. Add 3, then multiply by 4 each time. _____

   c) Start at 200. Add 25, then subtract 7 each time. _____

   d) Start at 4. Multiply by 8, then subtract 2 each time. _____

2. Write the next 4 terms in each pattern. Write each pattern rule.

   a) 460, 435, 410, 385, 360, _____, _____, _____, _____

   Pattern Rule: _____

   b) 7, 25, 79, 241, 727, _____, _____, _____, _____

   Pattern Rule: _____

   c) 12, 36, 84, 180, 372, _____, _____, _____, _____

   Pattern Rule: _____

   d) 8, 12, 24, 60, 168, _____, _____, _____, _____

   Pattern Rule: _____

3. Write the 8th term of each pattern.

   a) 1, 5, 33, 229, 1601, … _____   b) 12, 59, 294, 1469, 7344, … _____

   c) 15, 24, 42, 78, 150, … _____   d) 3, 19, 99, 499, 2499, … _____

Stretch Your Thinking ·

1. Write the first 6 terms of 2 different recursive patterns beginning with 2, 6. Then write each pattern rule.

   a) 2, 6, _____, _____, _____, _____

   Pattern Rule: _____

   b) 2, 6, _____, _____, _____, _____

   Pattern Rule: _____

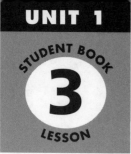
Patterns in Division

Quick Review

Divisibility Rules

A whole number is divisible by:	If:	Example:
2	the number is even	$2486 \div 2 = 1243$
3	the sum of the digits is divisible by 3	687: $6 + 8 + 7 = 21$ $21 \div 3 = 7$
4	the last 2 digits are divisible by 4	3572: $72 \div 4 = 18$
5	the last digit is 0 or 5	$7345 \div 5 = 1469$
6	the number is divisible by 2 and by 3	$90 \div 2 = 45$ $90 \div 3 = 30$ $90 \div 6 = 15$
8	the last 3 digits are divisible by 8	45 920: $920 \div 8 = 115$
9	the sum of the digits is divisible by 9	5868: $5 + 8 + 6 + 8 = 27$ $27 \div 9 = 3$
10	the last digit is 0	$2570 \div 10 = 257$

Try These

1. Write the numbers shown in the box that are divisible by:

   a) 10 _____

   b) 9 _____

   c) 3 _____

   d) 5 _____

   e) 4 _____

   f) 8 _____

2710	60	738
580	425	865
2823	142	640
4328	970	38
5512	7317	7592

Practice

1. **a)** Use the Venn diagram to sort
   these numbers:

7293	2486
576	981
765	840
644	3234
9638	371

   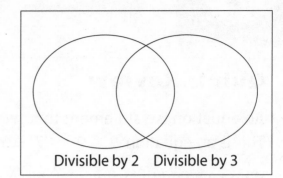

   Divisible by 2   Divisible by 3

   b) Add 1 more number to each
   section of the Venn diagram.

2. Write three 4-digit numbers that are divisible by:

   a) 3 _____   **b)** 4 _____

   c) 6 _____   **d)** 8 _____

   e) 9 _____   **f)** 10 _____

3. Roll 4 number cubes. Use the numbers rolled to form a 4-digit number.
   Record the number in the chart. Then tell by which numbers from 2 to 10
   your number is divisible.
   Repeat 4 more times.

Number	Divisible by

Stretch Your Thinking

Find a 4-digit number that is divisible by 2, by 3, by 4, by 9, and by 10.

_____

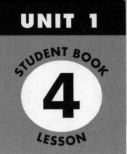
Solving Equations

Quick Review

An equation is a statement that two things are equal.
This is an equation: $9 \times 9 = 87 - 6$.

When we find the value of a missing number in an equation,
we **solve the equation**.
Here are 2 ways to find the missing number in an equation.

➤ Use guess and check.
Find the missing number.
$584 = \boxed{} - 121$

Guess 700: $700 - 121 = 579$
This difference is too low.

Guess 705: $705 - 121 = 584$
The missing number is 705.

➤ Use the inverse operation.
Solve this equation.
$\boxed{} \times 8 = 776$

Think division.
$776 \div 8 = 97$

So, $97 \times 8 = 776$
The solution is 97.

Try These

1. Find the missing number.

   a) ____ $+ 14 = 18$ b) $95 = $ ____ $- 44$ c) $19 \times$ ____ $= 76$

   d) ____ $- 36 = 14$ e) ____ $+ 4 = 37$ f) $22 - $ ____ $= 14$

   g) $25 + $ ____ $= 70$ h) ____ $\times 24 = 72$ i) $5 \times$ ____ $= 100$

2. Solve each equation.

   a) ____ $+ 14 = 7 + 7$ b) $9 \times 3 = 3 \times$ ____

   c) $12 + 9 = $ ____ $+ 3$ d) $6 \times$ ____ $= 9 \times 4$

   e) $52 - $ ____ $= 35 - 4$ f) $8 \times$ ____ $= 2 \times 16$

Solve each equation.

1. **a)** ____ + 3 = 37   **b)** ____ − 30 = 80   **c)** 480 = 8 × ____

   d) 84 = 107 − ____   **e)** 13 × ____ = 39   **f)** 345 ÷ ____ = 15

2. **a)** ____ − 4 = 13 − 3   **b)** 8 × 3 = 6 × ____   **c)** 35 + ____ = 17 + 19

   d) 88 ÷ 8 = 121 ÷ ____   **e)** 9 × ____ = 45 × 2   **f)** 942 − ____ = 800 − 250

3. Replace each □ and △ with a number to make an equation.
   Do this in 5 different ways.

   a) □ + △ = 287   **b)** □ + △ = 100

   _____   _____

   _____   _____

   _____   _____

   _____   _____

   _____   _____

4. Write an equation to model each problem. Solve each equation.

   a) Marjory bought 16 plums. After giving some to Shandar, she had
   11 plums left. How many plums did Marjory give to Shandar?

   _____

   _____

   b) Sylvester's rectangular garden is 28 m long and has an area of 392 m².
   What is the width of the garden?

   _____

   _____

Stretch Your Thinking . . . .

Suppose □ + △ = 247. If the value of □ increases by 17, how must the value
of △ change so that the equation is still true?

_____

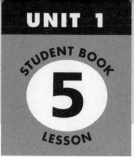

Exploring Integers

Quick Review

At Home At School

➤ A temperature greater than 0°C is positive.
We write: 15°C
We say: fifteen degrees Celsius

A temperature less than 0°C is negative.
We write: −15°C
We say: minus 15 degrees Celsius

➤ Numbers such as 15 and −15 are **integers**.
You can show integers on a number line.

A thermometer is a vertical number line.

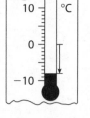

We extend a horizontal number line to the left of 0 to show negative numbers.

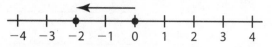

The thermometer shows −8°C.

The arrow represents −2.

➤ Negative numbers are always shown with a minus sign (−).
Positive numbers may or may not be shown with a plus sign (+).

➤ We use integers to represent different situations.
  • Tory saved $10. This can be represented as +$10, or $10.
  • Kim dove to a depth of 5 m. This can be represented as −5 m.

Try These . . . .

1. Write an integer to represent each situation.

   a) Violet earned $75 last week. _____

   b) It was fourteen degrees Celsius below zero. _____

   c) The frightened boy took 2 steps back. _____

   d) The helicopter rose to an altitude of 1500 m. _____

1. Write an integer to represent each situation.

   a) Ethanol freezes at minus 114°C. _____

   b) Tinotenda lost 4 kg. _____

   c) Lynne grew 3 cm this year. _____

   d) The Sipp family made $245 at their garage sale. _____

2. Describe a situation that could be represented by each integer.

   a) −14 _____

   b) +37 _____

   c) −3700 _____

   d) +284 _____

3. Write each explanation.

   a) If +7 represents 7 floors up, what does minus 3 represent?

   _____

   b) If −400 represents 400 m below sea level, what does +3000 represent?

   _____

   c) If +14 represents 14 steps forward, what does −8 represent?

   _____

   d) If −9 represents 9 points lost, what does +15 represent?

   _____

Stretch Your Thinking . . . .

Research to find examples of unusual temperatures, such as boiling and freezing points of various liquids, or temperatures on other planets. Record your findings.

_____

_____

_____

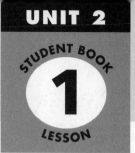

Exploring One Million

Quick Review

➤ One **million** is 1000 thousands.
Here are some benchmarks for 1 million.

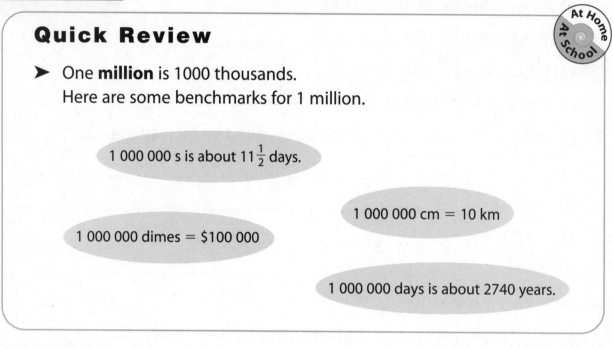

1 000 000 s is about $11\frac{1}{2}$ days.

1 000 000 cm = 10 km

1 000 000 dimes = $100 000

1 000 000 days is about 2740 years.

Try These

Show your work.

1. Suppose you save $100 a month. How many months would it take you to save $1 million?

2. In its lifetime, a ladybug can eat about 50 000 aphids.
    How many ladybugs would it take to eat about 1 million aphids?

3. How many days would it take to walk 1 million metres if you walked about 4000 m per day?

Name

1. Are there more than 1 million or less than 1 million:

   a) grains of sand on a beach? _____

   b) books in your classroom? _____

   c) blades of grass on a golf course? _____

2. How many of each would it take to make $1 million?

   a) $100 bills _____   b) $50 bills _____   c) $20 bills _____

   d) $10 bills _____   e) $5 bills _____   f) toonies _____

   g) quarters _____   h) dimes _____   i) nickels _____

3. Suppose you read 1000 pages a month. How long would it take you to finish reading 1 million pages?

   _____

4. How many boxes of paper clips would you need to get each number?

   a) 10 000 _____   b) 100 000 _____

   c) 500 000 _____   d) 1 000 000 _____

5. a) Suppose 1 bamboo skewer is about 30 cm long. How many skewers would it take to make a line 1 million centimetres long?

   _____

   b) How long would the line be in mm? _____

   In dm? _____   In m? _____   In km? _____

Stretch Your Thinking

Do you think many people live to be 1 million hours old? Explain how you know.

_____

_____

_____

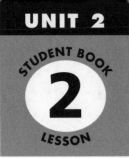

UNIT 2
STUDENT BOOK 2 LESSON

Understanding Large Numbers

Quick Review

➤ Here are some ways to represent the number 26 489 215.

Standard Form: 26 489 215

Words: twenty-six million four hundred eighty-nine thousand two hundred fifteen

Expanded Form:

20 000 000 + 6 000 000 + 400 000 + 80 000 + 9000 + 200 + 10 + 5

Number-Word Form: 26 million 489 thousand 215

Place-Value Chart:

Millions Period			Thousands Period			Units Period		
Hundreds	Tens	Ones	Hundreds	Tens	Ones	Hundreds	Tens	Ones
	2	6	4	8	9	2	1	5

➤ The place-value chart can be extended to the left to show greater whole numbers.

Trillions			Billions			Millions			Thousands			Units		
H	T	O	H	T	O	H	T	O	H	T	O	H	T	O

Try These

1. Write each number in standard form.

   a) 7 million 481 thousand 624 _____

   b) 3 000 000 000 + 200 000 000 + 600 000 + 20 000 + 9 _____

   c) four million six hundred sixty-two thousand eighty-two _____

2. Write the value of each underlined digit.

   a) 72 348 675 125 _____   b) 494 434 434 _____

14

1. Complete the chart.

Standard Form	Expanded Form	Number-Word Form
3 267 417		
	4 000 000 + 600 000 + 4000 + 90 + 2	
		625 million 227 thousand 282

2. Write each number in words.

   a) 62 430 021 _____

   _____

   b) 5 602 347 189 _____

   _____

   c) 25 482 617 _____

   _____

3. Find 2 large numbers in a newspaper or magazine.
   Write each number in as many ways as you can.

   a) _____

   _____

   b) _____

   _____

Stretch Your Thinking

Represent and describe the number 1 trillion in as many ways as you can.

_____

_____

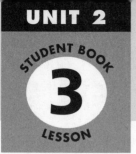

Comparing and Ordering Numbers

Quick Review

We can use place value to order numbers.

Order these numbers from greatest to least:

2 385 601   3 967 424   2 481 004

3 967 424 has 3 millions.
So, it is the greatest number.

Both 2 385 601 and 2 481 004 have 2 millions.
2 481 004 has 481 thousands.   2 385 601 has 385 thousands.
So, 2 481 004 > 2 385 601

So, 3 967 424 > 2 481 004 > 2 385 601
The numbers from greatest to least are:
3 967 424, 2 481 004, 2 385 601

Try These

1. Compare the numbers using > or <.

   a) 3 872 423 ☐ 7 001 326   b) 85 467 ☐ 125 736

   c) 29 614 327 ☐ 31 672 358   d) 4 673 426 004 ☐ 396 612 808

2. Order these numbers from least to greatest:

   1 004 672, 1 365 491, 955 672

   _____

3. Order these numbers from greatest to least:

   258 064 371, 258 153 427, 1 285 684 373

   _____

....

1. Play this game with a partner.
   You will need a paper bag containing 2 sets of cards with the digits 0 to 9.
   ➤ Draw a card from the bag.
     Record the digit in any space in the first row of your game board.
     Return the card to the bag.
   ➤ Take turns until each player fills all 7 spaces in a row.
   ➤ Compare your numbers.
     Write > or < in the box between your numbers.
     The player with the greater number wins a point.
   ➤ Play 3 more rounds.

Player A		Player B
___ ___ ___ ___ ___ ___ ___	☐	___ ___ ___ ___ ___ ___ ___
___ ___ ___ ___ ___ ___ ___	☐	___ ___ ___ ___ ___ ___ ___
___ ___ ___ ___ ___ ___ ___	☐	___ ___ ___ ___ ___ ___ ___
___ ___ ___ ___ ___ ___ ___	☐	___ ___ ___ ___ ___ ___ ___

2. a) Write your numbers from the game in order from least to greatest.

   _____

   b) Write your partner's numbers in order from greatest to least.

   _____

Stretch Your Thinking ....

1. The median in a set of numbers is the middle number when the numbers
   are arranged in order.
   Circle the median in each set of numbers.

   a) 210 001 020   b) 5 207 704   c) 7 685 391

      210 010 020   5 207 405   7 685 283

      210 010 100   5 801 409   7 685 299

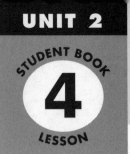

UNIT 2

STUDENT BOOK 4 LESSON

Exploring Multiples

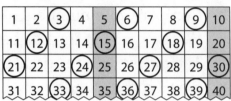

Quick Review

To find the **multiples** of a number, start at that number and count on by the number.

The multiples of 5 are:
5, 10, 15, 20, 25, 30, 35, 40, ...

The multiples of 3 are:
3, 6, 9, 12, 15, 18, 21, 24, 27, 30, 33, 36, 39, ...

1	2	③	4	5	⑥	7	8	⑨	10
11	⑫	13	14	⑮	16	17	⑱	19	20
㉑	22	23	㉔	25	26	㉗	28	29	㉚
31	32	㉝	34	35	㊱	37	38	㊴	40

15 and 30 appear in both lists.
They are **common multiples** of 5 and 3.

Each common multiple of 5 and 3 is divisible by 5 and by 3.

Try These

1. List the first 6 multiples of each number.

   a) 4 _____   b) 9 _____

   c) 25 _____   d) 6 _____

   e) 12 _____   f) 100 _____

2. Use the hundred chart.
   Colour the multiples of 7.
   Circle the multiples of 3.
   What are the common multiples
   of 7 and 3 on the chart?

   _____

1	2	3	4	5	6	7	8	9	10
11	12	13	14	15	16	17	18	19	20
21	22	23	24	25	26	27	28	29	30
31	32	33	34	35	36	37	38	39	40
41	42	43	44	45	46	47	48	49	50
51	52	53	54	55	56	57	58	59	60
61	62	63	64	65	66	67	68	69	70
71	72	73	74	75	76	77	78	79	80
81	82	83	84	85	86	87	88	89	90
91	92	93	94	95	96	97	98	99	100

Name_____

If a number is a multiple of a particular number that means it is divisible by that number.

1. Write the first 10 multiples of each pair of numbers.
   Circle the common multiples of each pair.

   a) 6: _____

      8: _____

   b) 4: _____

      7: _____

2. Sort these numbers in the Venn diagram.
   20, 33, 36, 88, 64, 48,
   68, 78, 84, 32, 76, 90,
   12, 54, 65, 42, 66, 102

   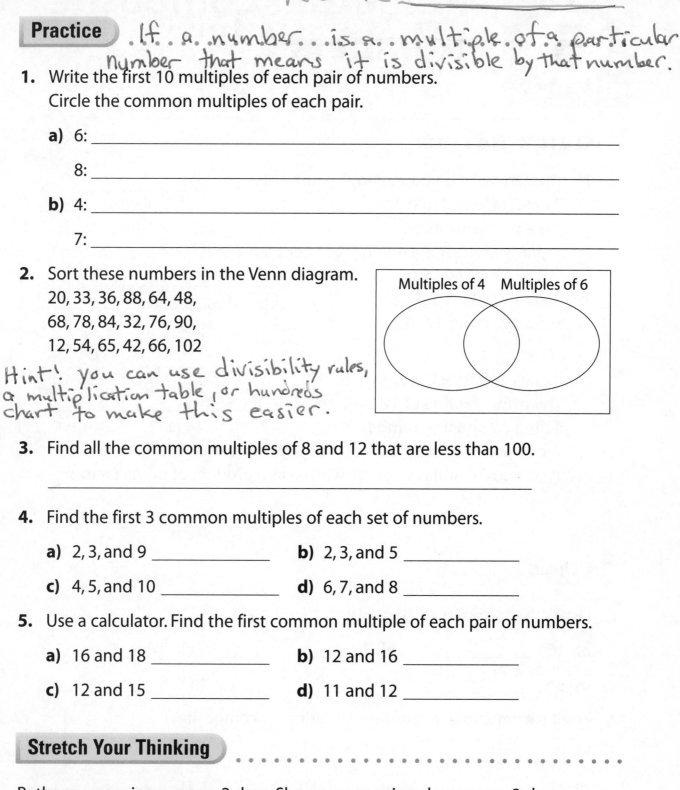

   Hint! you can use divisibility rules, a multiplication table, or hundreds chart to make this easier.

3. Find all the common multiples of 8 and 12 that are less than 100.

   _____

4. Find the first 3 common multiples of each set of numbers.

   a) 2, 3, and 9 _____   b) 2, 3, and 5 _____

   c) 4, 5, and 10 _____   d) 6, 7, and 8 _____

5. Use a calculator. Find the first common multiple of each pair of numbers.

   a) 16 and 18 _____   b) 12 and 16 _____

   c) 12 and 15 _____   d) 11 and 12 _____

Stretch Your Thinking . . . .

Bethany wears jeans every 2 days. She wears running shoes every 3 days.
If she wears jeans with running shoes on May 1, what are the next 3 dates
on which she will wear both jeans and running shoes?

_____

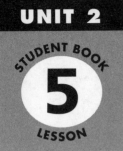

UNIT 2

STUDENT BOOK 5 LESSON

Prime and Composite Numbers

Quick Review

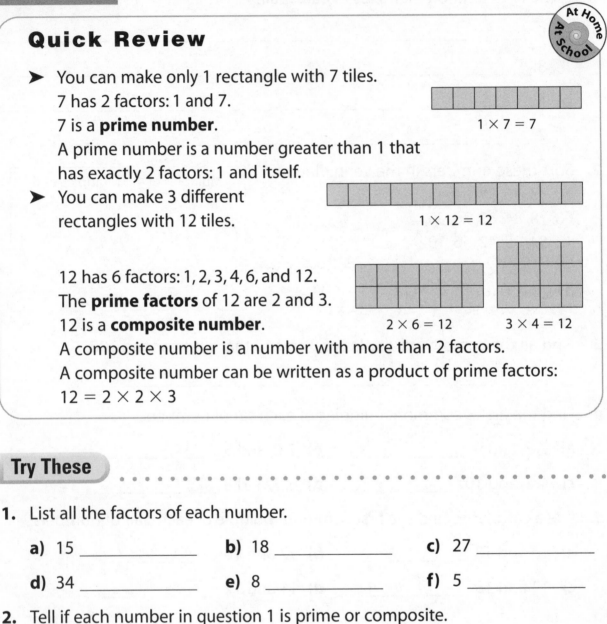

➤ You can make only 1 rectangle with 7 tiles.
7 has 2 factors: 1 and 7.
7 is a **prime number**.
A prime number is a number greater than 1 that has exactly 2 factors: 1 and itself.

$1 \times 7 = 7$

➤ You can make 3 different rectangles with 12 tiles.

$1 \times 12 = 12$

12 has 6 factors: 1, 2, 3, 4, 6, and 12.
The **prime factors** of 12 are 2 and 3.
12 is a **composite number**.
A composite number is a number with more than 2 factors.
A composite number can be written as a product of prime factors:
$12 = 2 \times 2 \times 3$

$2 \times 6 = 12$ $3 \times 4 = 12$

At Home At School

Try These •

1. List all the factors of each number.

    a) 15 _____   **b)** 18 _____   **c)** 27 _____

    d) 34 _____   **e)** 8 _____   **f)** 5 _____

2. Tell if each number in question 1 is prime or composite.

    a) _____   **b)** _____   **c)** _____

    d) _____   **e)** _____   **f)** _____

3. Write 2 numbers less than 50 that have exactly 3 factors.

    _____

1. Play this game with a partner.
   You will need 6 number cubes, each labelled 1 to 6.
   ➤ Each player's turn lasts until the total rolled on the number cubes
   is a prime number.
   The object of the game is to roll a prime number total using the least
   number of rolls.
   ➤ On each roll, you may choose to use from 2 to 6 number cubes.
   The number of rolls needed to reach a prime number is your score
   for that round.
   ➤ The player with the lower score at the end of 5 rounds wins.

2. Three numbers between 80 and 100 are prime numbers.

   What numbers are they? _____

3. Eight numbers between 31 and 41 are composite numbers.

   What numbers are they? _____

4. Use the table to sort the numbers from 30 to 50.

	Odd	**Even**
Prime		
Composite		

Write the ages of 6 relatives.
Tell whether each age is a prime number or a composite number.

_____

_____

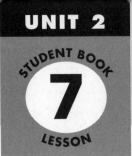

UNIT 2

STUDENT BOOK 7 LESSON

Using Mental Math

Quick Review

At Home At School

Here are some mental math strategies.

➤ Use compatible numbers.
Add: 30 + 62 + 70
30 + 62 + 70 = (30 + 70) + 62
= 100 + 62
= 162

Multiply: 2 × 14 × 50
2 × 14 × 50 = 14 × (2 × 50)
= 14 × 100
= 1400

➤ When no regrouping is needed, start from the left.
Subtract: 867 − 324
Think: 800 − 300 = 500
60 − 20 = 40
7 − 4 = 3
500 + 40 + 3 = 543

➤ Break one of the numbers apart.
Multiply: 4 × 36
4 × 36   = 4 × (30 + 6)
= (4 × 30) + (4 × 6)
= 120 + 24
= 144

Try These

Use mental math.

1. Add or subtract.

   a) 125 + 73 + 75 = _____   **b)** 983 − 421 = _____

   c) 86 + 20 + 14 = _____   **d)** 736 − 413 = _____

   e) 4376 − 2345 = _____   **f)** 40 + 125 + 60 = _____

2. Multiply.

   a) 8 × 37 = _____   **b)** 5 × 53 = _____   **c)** 2 × 78 = _____

   d) 9 × 69 = _____   **e)** 6 × 74 = _____   **f)** 5 × 26 = _____

   g) 2 × 18 × 50 = _____   **h)** 125 × 5 × 4 = _____   **i)** 20 × 9 × 20 = _____

22

Use mental math to solve each problem.
Match each answer to a number below the blanks to solve this riddle.

Why did the teacher
wear sunglasses
to school?

$45 + 17 + 55 =$ _____ (S) $876 - 544 =$ _____ (E)

$297 - 146 =$ _____ (G) $69 \times 6 =$ _____ (U)

$5 \times 13 \times 20 =$ _____ (X) $2 \times 52 \times 50 =$ _____ (B)

$7 \times 29 =$ _____ (H) $125 + 475 + 32 =$ _____ (Y)

$352 + 446 =$ _____ (A) $5476 - 2345 =$ _____ (T)

$36 \times 9 =$ _____ (R) $500 \times 8 \times 2 =$ _____ (C)

$180 + 220 + 26 =$ _____ (L) $24 \times 5 \times 2 =$ _____ (I)

$817 - 205 =$ _____ (V) $9 \times 71 =$ _____ (W)

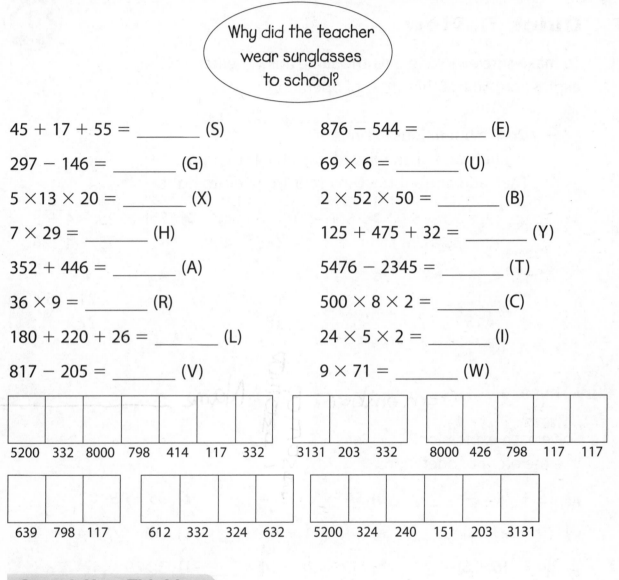

5200	332	8000	798	414	117	332

3131	203	332

8000	426	798	117	117

639	798	117

612	332	324	632

5200	324	240	151	203	3131

Stretch Your Thinking

Describe two different ways to find $2 \times 50 \times 25$ using mental math.

_____

_____

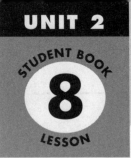
Order of Operations

Quick Review

At Home At School

To make sure everyone gets the same answer when solving an expression, we use this order of operations:

> • Do the operations in brackets.
> • Multiply and divide, in order, from left to right.
> • Then add and subtract, in order, from left to right.

➤ Solve: $12 + 20 \div 5$
$12 + 20 \div 5$
$= 12 + 4$
$= 16$

➤ Solve: $9 \times (6 - 4)$
$9 \times (6 - 4)$
$= 9 \times 2$
$= 18$

➤ Solve: $25 - 4 + 6$
$25 - 4 + 6$
$= 21 + 6$
$= 27$

Try These .... Remember BEDMAS Name _____

1. Solve each expression.
   Use the order of operations.

   a) $15 + 7 \times 2 =$ _____   **b)** $34 - 6 \div 3 =$ _____   **c)** $35 + 15 \times 2 =$ _____

   d) $30 \div (2 + 3) =$ _____   **e)** $44 \div 11 + 4 =$ _____   **f)** $(14 \div 7) \times 4 =$ _____

   g) $24 + (16 \div 8) =$ _____   **h)** $(17 + 2) - 14 =$ _____   **i)** $3 \times 9 - 4 =$ _____

2. _____

   a) $2 \times 9 - 3 + 4 =$ _____   **b)** $5 + 150 \div 25 =$ _____

   c) $30 + 30 \div 6 =$ _____   **d)** $(8 \times 9) - (8 \times 8) =$ _____

   e) $24 \div 12 \times 9 =$ _____   **f)** $(200 + 400) \times 2 =$ _____

   g) $18 \div 2 \times 2 =$ _____   **h)** $4 \times (3 \times 5) =$ _____

   i) $12 + 6 - 2 =$ _____   **j)** $(50 + 100) \times 2 - 100 =$ _____

1. Solve each expression.

   a) $48 \div 12 \div 2 =$ _____   **b)** $8 \times (10 - 4) =$ _____   **c)** $28 - 12 \div 4 =$ _____

   d) $7 \times (3 + 2) =$ _____   **e)** $16 \div 2 \times 9 =$ _____   **f)** $15 \div (3 \times 5) =$ _____

2. Use brackets to make each number sentence true.

   a) $2 \times 3 + 6 = 18$ **b)** $20 \times 15 - 2 = 260$

   c) $5 + 4 \div 3 = 3$ **d)** $12 + 10 \div 11 = 2$

   e) $6 + 8 \div 2 = 10$ **f)** $5 \times 4 \div 2 = 10$

3. Write a number sentence to show the order of operations you use to solve each problem.

   a) Sandar bought four bags of chips at $2.99 each.
   She used a $2.00 coupon to pay part of the cost.
   How much did Sandar pay for the chips?

   _____

   b) The decorating committee needs 3 balloons for each of 15 tables.
   They also need 20 balloons for each of the 4 walls of the room.
   How many balloons does the committee need?

   _____

Stretch Your Thinking . . . .

You and 3 friends order a pizza, 4 large drinks, and a loaf of cheese bread.
You split the cost evenly with your friends.
What order of operations would you use to find out
how much each person should pay?

_____

_____

_____

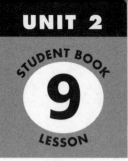
Adding and Subtracting Whole Numbers

Quick Review

At Home At School

We can use place value to add and subtract.

➤ Add: 327 + 465 + 308 + 194

Add the ones. Regroup.	Add the tens. Regroup.	Add the hundreds. Regroup.	Estimate to check.
2	12	1 2	
32**7**	**3**27	**3**27	300
46**5**	**4**65	**4**65	500
30**8**	**3**08	**3**08	300
+ 19**4**	+ **1**94	+ **1**94	+ 200
4	**9**4	**12**94	1300

➤ Subtract: 17 294 − 5736

Regroup the tens. Subtract the ones. Subtract the tens.	Regroup the thousands. Subtract the hundreds. Subtract the thousands.	Add to check.
8 14	6 12 8 14	1 1
1729̶4̶	1̶7̶2̶9̶4̶	5736
− 5736	− 5736	+ 11558
58	11558	17294

Try These

1. Add and then estimate to check. Or, subtract and then add to check.

a)
```
   341
   285
   673
 + 285      + ____
```

b)
```
   714
   356
   221
 + 387      + ____
```

c)
```
  23876
 − 1957     + ____
```

1. Add. Estimate to check.

   a) 573   **b)** 731   **c)** 579
         695   184   804
         814   226   89
     + 238 + ___   + 638 + ___   + 631 + ___

2. Subtract. Use addition to check.

   a) 5609   **b)** 25173   **c)** 91272
     − 2738 + ___   − 8585 + ___   − 4387 + ___

3. The table shows attendance at Camp Tekawitha this summer.

   a) How many children attended the camp?

   _____

   b) Last year, the total attendance at the camp was 1572.
   How many more or fewer children attended the camp this summer?

   _____

Camp Tekawitha Attendance	
Age Group	Number of Children
5−7	342
8−10	525
11−13	428
14−16	137

4. The difference of two 4-digit numbers is 5639. What might the numbers be?

   _____

Stretch Your Thinking

The sum of four consecutive 3-digit numbers is 3990.
What are the 4 numbers?

_____

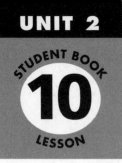
Multiplying Whole Numbers

At Home
At School

Quick Review

Here are 2 ways to multiply 236×24.

➤ Break the numbers apart.

	236	$(200 + 30 + 6)$
Multiply:	$\times\ 24$	$(20 + 4)$
4×6	24	
4×30	120	
4×200	800	
20×6	120	
20×30	600	
20×200	4000	
Add:	5664	

➤ Use a short way to multiply.

	236
Multiply:	$\times\ 24$
236×4	944
236×20	4720
Add:	5664

You can check by dividing: $5664 \div 236 = 24$
So, 5664 is the correct answer.

Try These •

1. Multiply.

    a)   324   **b)**   509   **c)**   628   **d)**   404

        $\times\ 25$ $\times\ 37$ $\times\ 73$ $\times\ 42$

2. Use a calculator and division to check your answers for question 1.

    a) _____ ÷ _____ = _____   **b)** _____ ÷ _____ = _____

    c) _____ ÷ _____ = _____   **d)** _____ ÷ _____ = _____

1. Play this game with a partner.
   You will need 2 number cubes, each labelled 1 to 6.

   ➤ Take turns.
      Roll the number cubes.
      Use the numbers on the cubes to make a 2-digit number.
      Choose a number from the game board and multiply the number
      by your 2-digit number.
      Record the product on paper.
   ➤ Keep a running total of your products.
      If you go over 150 000, the game is over and the other player wins.
   ➤ You may stop rolling and "hold" with your total when you get close
      to 150 000.
      Then the player closer to 150 000 wins.

367	489	526	193	204	200
309	631	145	417	723	499
154	312	418	102	267	120

2. Estimate the product of:

   a) 29×498 _____

   b) 81×204 _____

   c) 97×350 _____

   d) 48×500 _____

Stretch Your Thinking ·

Use the digits 1, 3, 5, 7, and 9 to make a 3-digit number and a 2-digit number
that will give the least product.
Show your work.

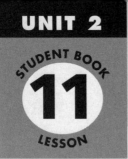
Dividing by a 2-Digit Number

Quick Review

Here is one way to divide 2485 seeds into 15 equal groups.
Put each listed amount into each group, then subtract: $15\overline{)2485}$

➤ 100 seeds 15×100

➤ 50 seeds 15×50

➤ 10 seeds 15×10

➤ 5 seeds 15×5

$$
\begin{array}{r|r}
15\overline{)2485} & \\
-1500 & 100 \\
\hline
985 & \\
-\ 750 & 50 \\
\hline
235 & \\
-\ 150 & 10 \\
\hline
85 & \\
-\ \ 75 & +\ 5 \\
\hline
10 & 165 \\
\end{array}
$$

$2485 \div 15 = 165 \text{ R}10$

To check the answer, multiply 165
by 15 and then add the leftover 10:

$$
\begin{array}{r}
165 \\
\times\ \ 15 \\
\hline
825 \\
+\ 1650 \\
\hline
2475 \\
\end{array}
$$

$2475 + 10 = 2485$

At Home
At School

Try These •

1. Divide.

a) $33\overline{)4532}$

b) $19\overline{)3947}$

c) $31\overline{)2367}$

1. Divide.

   a) 24)3685   **b)** 37)8536   **c)** 43)5679

2. Multiply to check each answer in question 1.

   a)   **b)**   **c)**

3. Complete each table.

Dividend	Divisor	Quotient
2357	17	
	24	16 R7
	33	170 R19
5084	49	

Dividend	Divisor	Quotient
	21	347
1836	11	
	26	24 R3
3625		25

Stretch Your Thinking . . . .

Make this division sentence true: _____ ÷ _____ = 25 R7

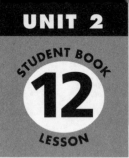

Another Method for Dividing

Quick Review

Divide: 46)6375

➤ Use place value to divide.

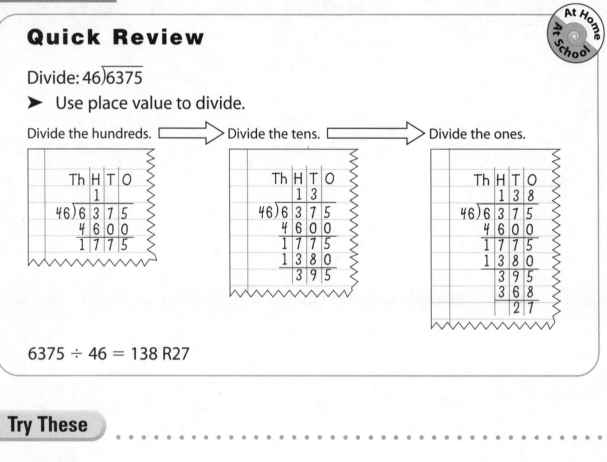

Divide the hundreds. ⟹ Divide the tens. ⟹ Divide the ones.

6375 ÷ 46 = 138 R27

Try These

1. Divide.

a) 37)4963   b) 41)3674   c) 25)1946   d) 18)1536

Practice . . . .

1. Divide. Then multiply to check.

   a) 84)7639

   b) 57)3891

   c) 27)2937

   d) 48)6739

2. A theatre has 5332 seats arranged in 86 equal rows.
   How many seats are in each row?

   _____

   _____

3. What number, when multiplied by 50, gives a product of 2150?

   _____

   _____

Stretch Your Thinking . . . .

Find the missing digits of the dividend. Then divide.

           33 R19
      53)1___

Name _____

Investigating Angles

At Home At School

Quick Review

➤ Some angles are equal to or greater than 180°.

Straight Angle

180°

Reflex Angle

between 180° and 360°

Angle in One Complete Turn

360°

➤ You can use a 360° protractor to measure a reflex angle.
Place the protractor on the angle.
Use the inside scale.
This angle measures 270°.

270°

Try These

1. Tell whether each angle is acute, right, obtuse, straight, or reflex.

   a)

   b)

   c)

   _____   _____   _____

2. Measure each angle in question 1.

   a) _____   b) _____   c) _____

Name

Reflex Angle

1. Use a protractor to measure each angle.

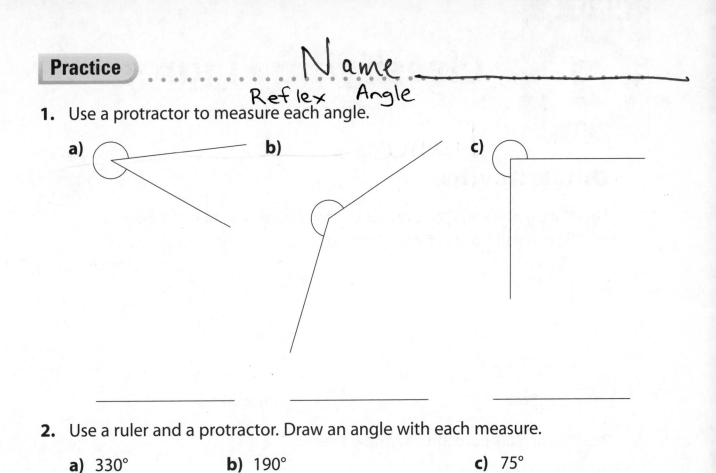

a)   b)   c)

_____   _____   _____

2. Use a ruler and a protractor. Draw an angle with each measure.

   a) 330°   b) 190°   c) 75°

Stretch Your Thinking

Draw a reflex angle.
Then draw a line to divide the reflex angle
into 2 angles of the same size.

Classifying Figures

Name

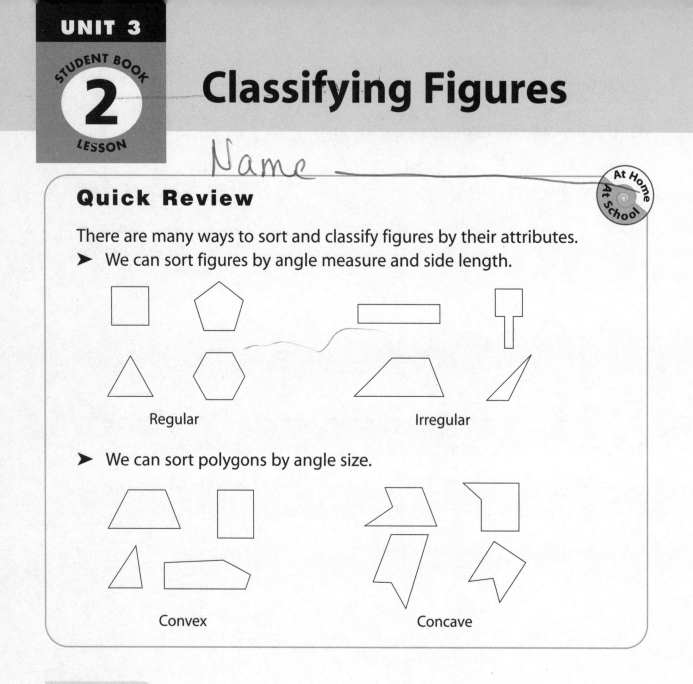

Quick Review

There are many ways to sort and classify figures by their attributes.

➤ We can sort figures by angle measure and side length.

Regular   Irregular

➤ We can sort polygons by angle size.

Convex   Concave

Try These . . . .

1. Use the Venn diagram to sort the figures.

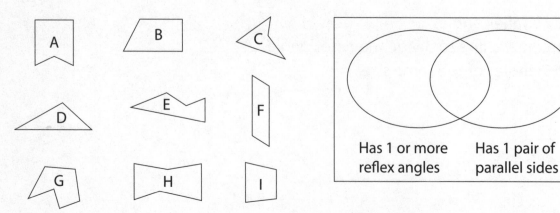

Has 1 or more reflex angles   Has 1 pair of parallel sides

1. Use the dot paper. Sketch 2 different figures for each set of clues.

   a) I have one reflex angle and 3 acute angles.

   · · · · · · · · · · · · · · · ·
   · · · · · · · · · · · · · · · ·
   · · · · · · · · · · · · · · · ·
   · · · · · · · · · · · · · · · ·
   · · · · · · · · · · · · · · · ·
   · · · · · · · · · · · · · · · ·
   · · · · · · · · · · · · · · · ·

   b) I have two pairs of parallel sides. None of my angles is 90°.

   · · · · · · · · · · · · · · · ·
   · · · · · · · · · · · · · · · ·
   · · · · · · · · · · · · · · · ·
   · · · · · · · · · · · · · · · ·
   · · · · · · · · · · · · · · · ·
   · · · · · · · · · · · · · · · ·
   · · · · · · · · · · · · · · · ·

   c) I have 5 sides. All of my angles are less than 180°.

   · · · · · · · · · · · · · · · ·
   · · · · · · · · · · · · · · · ·
   · · · · · · · · · · · · · · · ·
   · · · · · · · · · · · · · · · ·
   · · · · · · · · · · · · · · · ·
   · · · · · · · · · · · · · · · ·
   · · · · · · · · · · · · · · · ·

   d) I have 2 right angles, 2 acute angles, and 1 reflex angle.

   · · · · · · · · · · · · · · · ·
   · · · · · · · · · · · · · · · ·
   · · · · · · · · · · · · · · · ·
   · · · · · · · · · · · · · · · ·
   · · · · · · · · · · · · · · · ·
   · · · · · · · · · · · · · · · ·
   · · · · · · · · · · · · · · · ·

Stretch Your Thinking . . . .

Describe this polygon in as many ways as you can.

_____

_____

_____

_____

_____

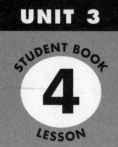
Constructing Figures

Quick Review

You can use a ruler and a protractor to construct square JKLM, with side lengths 2 cm.

Step 1
Use a ruler to draw segment KL 2 cm long.

Step 2
At K, use a protractor to measure 90°.
Draw segment KJ 2 cm long.

Step 3
Use a protractor to measure 90° at L.
Draw segment LM 2 cm long.

Step 4
Draw line segment JM.
Label each measure.

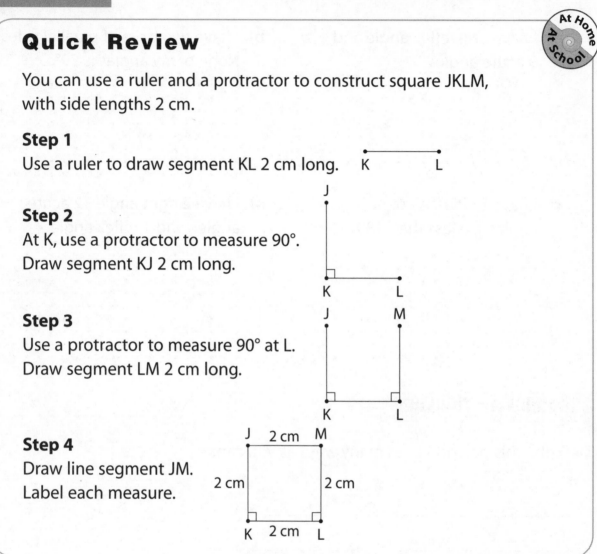

Try These

1. Use a ruler and a protractor.
   Construct rectangle ABCD with length
   5 cm and width 4 cm.

Name

Use a ruler and a protractor or a compass.

1. Construct parallelogram JKLM
   with KL = JM = 6 cm,
   JK = LM = 3 cm, ∠JKL = 70°,
   and ∠KLM = 110°.

2. **a)** Construct trapezoid NOPQ
   with sides OP = 7 cm,
   ON = QP = 4 cm, and
   ∠NOP = ∠OPQ = 60°.

   b) What is the length of NQ?

   _____

3. Construct △UVW with side lengths
   UV = 5 cm, VW = 7 cm, and
   UW = 4 cm. Measure the angles.

   ∠U = _____

   ∠V = _____

   ∠W = _____

Stretch Your Thinking

Construct two different
convex quadrilaterals.
Each quadrilateral must
have no equal sides and
1 angle that measures 130°.

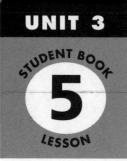

Nets of Objects

Quick Review

A net shows all the faces of an object.
Each face is joined to another face along one edge.
The net can be folded to make the object.

➤ This is *not* a net for a cube.
If this diagram were folded,
2 squares would overlap and
1 side would not have a face.

➤ This is a net for a triangular prism.
It has 3 congruent rectangles and
2 congruent equilateral triangles.
If this diagram were folded,
it would be a triangular prism.

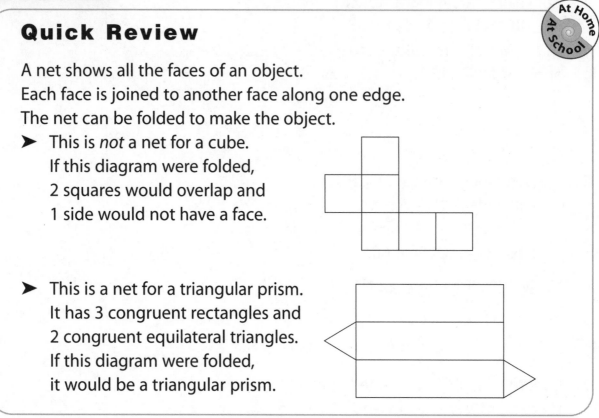

Try These

1. Identify the object that has each net.

   a)

   b)

   c)

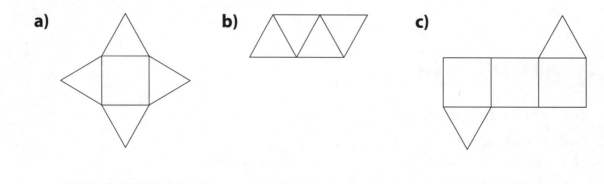

_____   _____   _____

Name

1. Sketch a net for each object.
   Use hatch marks to show which sides have the same length.

   a) a pentagonal pyramid   b) a rectangular prism

2. Identify the object that has each set of faces. Sketch the faces to form a net.

   a) 1 regular hexagon and   b) 6 congruent squares
      6 congruent triangles

      _____   _____

Stretch Your Thinking

Sketch a net for a cube on the grid.
Write the letters M, A, T, and H on
4 faces of the net so that if you
fold the net, you could read the
word MATH.

Illustrating Objects

Name _____

Quick Review

A drawing on triangular dot paper is called an **isometric drawing**.

➤ Here is one way to make an isometric drawing of this object.

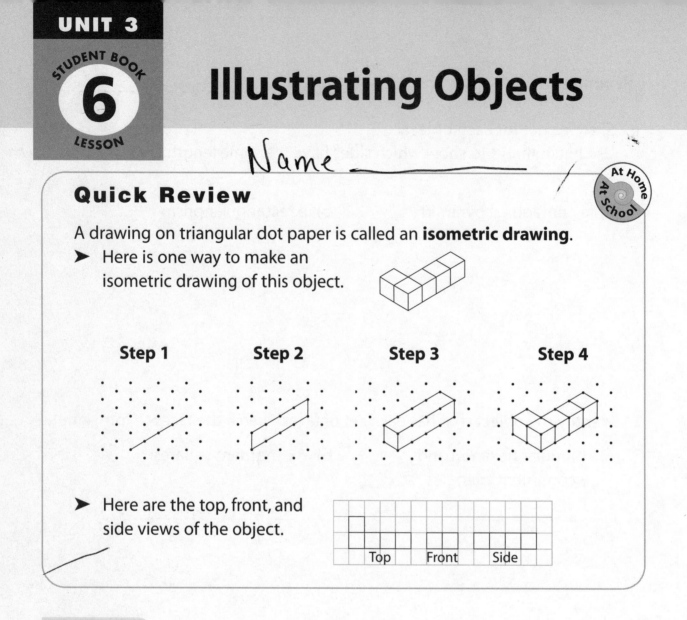

Step 1   **Step 2**   **Step 3**   **Step 4**

➤ Here are the top, front, and side views of the object.

Top   Front   Side

Try These

1. Make an isometric drawing of each object.

a)

b)

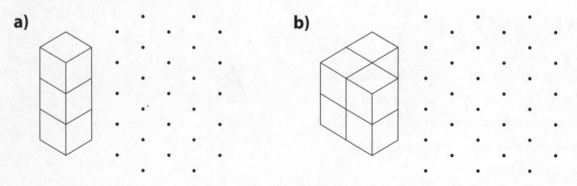

1. Make an isometric drawing of each object.

   a)

   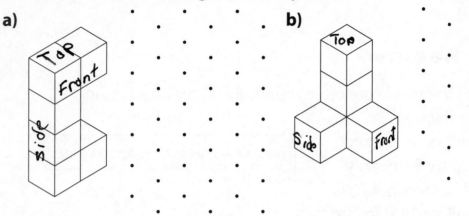

   b)

2. Draw the top, front, and side views of each object in question 1.

   a)

   b)

3. Draw the object for this set of views.

   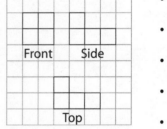

Stretch Your Thinking

Draw an object that
is not a prism.
Then draw the top,
front, and side views.

UNIT 4

STUDENT BOOK

1

LESSON

Numbers in the Media

At Home
At School

Quick Review

Numbers in the media are often rounded and reported using decimals or fractions.

➤ $32.7 million is the cost rounded to the nearest tenth of a million dollars. $32.7 million in standard form is $32 700 000.

> New Library to Cost $32.7 Million

➤ $2\frac{1}{2}$ billion is 2 billion plus 500 millions.
$2\frac{1}{2}$ billion in standard form is 2 500 000 000.

> Fossil Believed to Be $2\frac{1}{2}$ Billion Years Old

➤ $3.75 million is $3 million plus $0.75 million.
$0.75 million is $750 000.
$3.75 million in standard form is $3 750 000.

> Woman Wins $3.75 Million in Lottery

Try These

1. Write each number in standard form.

   a) $5\frac{1}{2}$ million _____

   b) 1.25 million _____

   c) 6.4 million _____

   d) $2\frac{3}{4}$ billion _____

2. Write each number as it might appear in a newspaper headline.

   a) 42 400 000 _____

   b) 15 250 000 _____

   c) 3 500 000 _____

   d) 7 800 000 _____

44

1. Write each number in standard form.

   a) 8.9 billion _____

   b) $7\frac{1}{4}$ million _____

   c) 6.2 million _____

   d) $6\frac{1}{2}$ million _____

2. Use decimals. Round each number to the nearest hundredth of a million.

   a) 5 672 848 _____

   b) 7 842 395 _____

   c) 2 555 427 _____

   d) 16 514 320 _____

3. Rewrite each number in as many ways as you can.

   a) 5 250 000 _____

   _____

   b) $2\frac{3}{4}$ million _____

   _____

   c) 42 500 000 _____

   _____

4. Make up 3 newspaper headlines with large numbers.

   a) _____

   b) _____

   c) _____

5. Write each number in question 4 in standard form.

   a) _____

   b) _____

   c) _____

Stretch Your Thinking

Research to find the population of Canada.
Write the number in as many ways as you can.

_____

_____

_____

Name _____

Exploring Thousandths

At Home
At School

Quick Review

➤ Numbers with tenths, hundredths, and thousandths can be written as decimals.

$\frac{3}{10}$ 0.3

three tenths

$1\frac{7}{100}$ 1.07

one and seven hundredths

$\frac{213}{1000}$ 0.213

two hundred thirteen thousandths

➤ You can use a place-value chart to show decimals.

Tens	Ones	•	Tenths	Hundredths	Thousandths
	4	•	6	2	3

➤ You can write decimals in expanded form.
   4.623 = 4 ones + 6 tenths + 2 hundredths + 3 thousandths
        = 4 + 0.6 + 0.02 + 0.003

Try These

1. Write each number as a decimal.

   a) $\frac{7}{100}$ _____

   b) $2\frac{14}{1000}$ _____

   c) $32\frac{19}{100}$ _____

   d) $5\frac{6}{1000}$ _____

   e) $216\frac{374}{1000}$ _____

   f) $\frac{108}{1000}$ _____

2. Write each decimal in expanded form.

   a) 0.405 _____

   b) 84.007 _____

3. Write each number in words.

   a) 0.234 _____

   b) 17.637 _____

1. Record each number in the place-value chart.

    a) 76 thousandths   **b)** 316 and 536 thousandths

    c) 185 thousandths   **d)** 93 and 3 thousandths

	Hundreds	Tens	Ones	•	Tenths	Hundredths	Thousandths
a)				•			
b)				•			
c)				•			
d)				•			

2. Write each number as a fraction or a mixed number.

    a) 3.047 _____   **b)** 62.354 _____   **c)** 0.739 _____

    d) 0.001 _____   **e)** 2.72 _____   **f)** 1.506 _____

3. Write each number in question 2 in expanded form.

    a) _____   **b)** _____

    c) _____   **d)** _____

    e) _____   **f)** _____

4. Write each number as a decimal.

    a) $2\frac{9}{1000}$ _____   **b)** $17\frac{6}{100}$ _____   **c)** $\frac{85}{1000}$ _____

    d) $5\frac{25}{1000}$ _____   **e)** $\frac{367}{1000}$ _____   **f)** $\frac{8}{1000}$ _____

Stretch Your Thinking ·

Use the digits 0, 2, 3, and 6.
Make a number that is greater than 1 but less than 4.
Find as many numbers as you can.

_____

_____

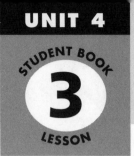

Comparing and Ordering Decimals

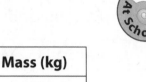

Quick Review

The table shows the masses of Henry's 3 kittens.

Kitten	Mass (kg)
Foofoo	0.395
Quigley	0.364
Oscar	0.391

Here are 2 ways to order the pets from least to greatest mass.

➤ Use a place-value chart.

Ones	•	Tenths	Hundredths	Thousandths
0	•	3	9	5
0	•	3	6	4
0	•	3	9	1

All 3 numbers have 0 ones and 3 tenths.
0.364 has the least hundredths, so it is the least number.
0.395 has the greatest number of thousandths, so it is the greatest.

The pets in order from least to greatest mass are: Quigley, Oscar, Foofoo.

➤ Use a number line.

```
                                      0.364      0.391 0.395
|++++++++++|++++++++++|++++++++++|++++++++++|++++++++++|++++++++++|++++++++++|++++++++++|+++•++++|++++++++++|+•++•+|
0.30 0.31 0.32 0.33 0.34 0.35 0.36 0.37 0.38 0.39 0.40
```

Reading numbers from left to right gives the masses from least to greatest.

Try These . . . .

1. Use >, <, or = to make each statement true.

   a) 0.457 _____ 0.406   **b)** 17.63 _____ 17.630   **c)** 5.976 _____ 6.0

2. Order the numbers from greatest to least.

   a) 0.36, 0.371, 0.329 _____   **b)** 2.76, 5.3, 2.485 _____

1. Play this game with a partner.
   You will need 2 sets of 10 cards numbered 0 to 9, in a paper bag.
   ➤ Take turns drawing a card from the bag.
     Record the digit in any space in the first row of your game board.
     Return the card to the bag.
   ➤ Continue until all 4 spaces in a row are filled.
   ➤ Compare your numbers using > or <.
   ➤ The player with the greater number wins a point.
   ➤ Play 4 more rounds.
     The player with the higher score wins.

Player A		Player B
___ . ___ ___ ___	☐	___ . ___ ___ ___
___ . ___ ___ ___	☐	___ . ___ ___ ___
___ . ___ ___ ___	☐	___ . ___ ___ ___
___ . ___ ___ ___	☐	___ . ___ ___ ___
___ . ___ ___ ___	☐	___ . ___ ___ ___

2. **a)** Write your numbers from the game in order from greatest to least.

   _____

   b) Write your partner's numbers from the game in order from least
   to greatest.

   _____

Stretch Your Thinking

Write all the numbers from the game in order from least to greatest.

_____

_____

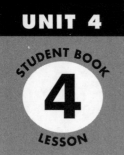
Rounding Decimals

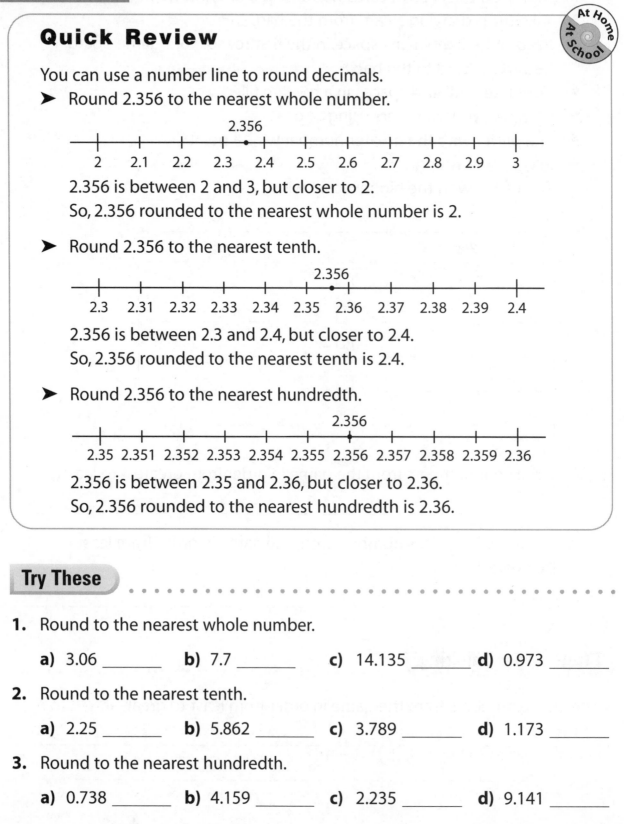

Quick Review

You can use a number line to round decimals.

➤ Round 2.356 to the nearest whole number.

2.356

| | | | | | | | | | | |
2   2.1   2.2   2.3   2.4   2.5   2.6   2.7   2.8   2.9   3

2.356 is between 2 and 3, but closer to 2.
So, 2.356 rounded to the nearest whole number is 2.

➤ Round 2.356 to the nearest tenth.

2.356

2.3   2.31   2.32   2.33   2.34   2.35   2.36   2.37   2.38   2.39   2.4

2.356 is between 2.3 and 2.4, but closer to 2.4.
So, 2.356 rounded to the nearest tenth is 2.4.

➤ Round 2.356 to the nearest hundredth.

2.356

2.35 2.351 2.352 2.353 2.354 2.355 2.356 2.357 2.358 2.359 2.36

2.356 is between 2.35 and 2.36, but closer to 2.36.
So, 2.356 rounded to the nearest hundredth is 2.36.

Try These

1. Round to the nearest whole number.

   a) 3.06 _____ b) 7.7 _____ c) 14.135 _____ d) 0.973 _____

2. Round to the nearest tenth.

   a) 2.25 _____ b) 5.862 _____ c) 3.789 _____ d) 1.173 _____

3. Round to the nearest hundredth.

   a) 0.738 _____ b) 4.159 _____ c) 2.235 _____ d) 9.141 _____

1. Do this activity with a partner.
   You will need a set of cards labelled 0 to 9, a penny, and a number cube labelled WN (whole number), T (tenths), H (hundredths), WN, T, H.
   ➤ Player A: Shuffle the number cards.
     Draw 4 cards and use them to form a decimal number with thousandths. Use the penny as the decimal point. Record the number in the table.
   ➤ Player B: Roll the number cube.
     Round Player A's number to the place rolled.
   ➤ Continue for 9 more numbers. Switch roles at each turn.

Decimal Number	Rounded Number	Decimal Number	Rounded Number

2. Round each number to the nearest whole number, the nearest tenth, the nearest hundredth.

   a) 5.678 _____ _____ _____

   b) 0.437 _____ _____ _____

   c) 2.435 _____ _____ _____

   d) 7.103 _____ _____ _____

Stretch Your Thinking

Use the digits 0, 2, 5, and 8. Write a decimal that will round up if rounded to the nearest whole number, round down if rounded to the nearest tenth, and round up if rounded to the nearest hundredth.

_____

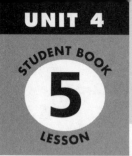
Estimating Sums and Differences

Quick Review

Here are 3 ways to estimate $4.548 + 2.417$.

➤ Round each decimal to the nearest whole number:
$5 + 2 = 7$

➤ Round only 1 decimal to the nearest whole number:
$5 + 2.417 = 7.417$

➤ Round each decimal to the nearest tenth or hundredth:
$4.5 + 2.4 = 6.9$
$4.55 + 2.42 = 6.97$

Here are 2 ways to estimate $4.538 - 2.417$.

➤ Round the second decimal to the nearest whole number:
$4.538 - 2 = 2.538$

➤ Round both decimals to the nearest tenth or hundredth:
$4.5 - 2.4 = 2.1$
$4.54 - 2.42 = 2.12$

Try These

1. Estimate each sum.

    a) $2.54 + 7.16$

    b) $4.197 + 3.864$

    c) $0.765 + 1.295$

    d) $5.765 + 3.189$

    e) $0.473 + 1.697$

    f) $2.008 + 3.801$

2. Estimate each difference.

    a) $7.546 - 3.518$

    b) $2.476 - 1.555$

    c) $7.9 - 3.267$

    d) $3.204 - 0.938$

    e) $1.497 - 0.126$

    f) $12.094 - 8.259$

Practice

1. Estimate each sum or difference.

   a) 27.6 + 49.23

   _____

   b) 16.257 − 9.396

   _____

   c) 4.875 − 2.93

   _____

   d) 7.596 + 2.17

   _____

   e) 13.123 − 6.959

   _____

   f) 10.67 + 7.834

   _____

2. a) Joline bought a pair of skates for $79.95.
      She also bought a pullover for $45.25.
      Estimate the total cost of Joline's purchases. _____

   b) Estimate how much more Joline paid for the skates than the pullover.

      _____

3. The table shows the masses of five puppies.

   a) Estimate the combined masses of:

      Brutus and Zeus _____

      Tawny and Zena _____

      Zeus and Zara _____

      Zara and Tawny _____

   b) Estimate the difference in masses of:

      Zara and Zena _____

      Brutus and Zeus _____

      Tawny and Zara _____

      The heaviest and lightest puppies _____

Masses of Puppies	
Name	**Mass (kg)**
Brutus	1.106
Tawny	0.992
Zara	0.935
Zena	0.791
Zeus	1.276

4. Circle the better estimate.

   a) 3.549 + 6.831   10 or 11

   b) 4.316 − 0.135   3 or 4

Stretch Your Thinking

Estimate the combined mass of the five puppies.

_____

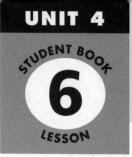

UNIT 4

Adding and Subtracting Decimals

STUDENT BOOK
6
LESSON

Quick Review

➤ You can use place value to add 5.763 and 3.949.

Step 1: Estimate.

Round 3.949 to 4.
Add: 5.763 + 4 = 9.763

Step 2: Add as you would with whole numbers.

$$\begin{array}{r} \overset{1\ 1\ 1}{5.763} \\ +\ 3.949 \\ \hline 9.712 \end{array}$$

9.712 is close to the estimate, so the answer is reasonable.

➤ You can use place value to subtract 3.949 from 5.763.

Step 1: Estimate.

Round 3.949 to 4.
Subtract 5.763 − 4 = 1.763

Step 2: Subtract as you would with whole numbers.

$$\begin{array}{r} \overset{4\ \ 17\ 5\ 13}{\cancel{5.763}} \\ -\ 3.949 \\ \hline 1.814 \end{array}$$

1.814 is close to the estimate, so the answer is reasonable.

Try These

1. Add.

   a) $\begin{array}{r} 4.521 \\ +\ 3.097 \\ \hline \end{array}$

   b) $\begin{array}{r} 2.168 \\ +\ 0.948 \\ \hline \end{array}$

   c) $\begin{array}{r} 7.169 \\ +\ 8.473 \\ \hline \end{array}$

   d) $\begin{array}{r} 6.704 \\ +\ 0.491 \\ \hline \end{array}$

2. Subtract.

   a) $\begin{array}{r} 9.732 \\ -\ 0.489 \\ \hline \end{array}$

   b) $\begin{array}{r} 6.371 \\ -\ 1.098 \\ \hline \end{array}$

   c) $\begin{array}{r} 4.152 \\ -\ 4.097 \\ \hline \end{array}$

   d) $\begin{array}{r} 3.652 \\ -\ 1.984 \\ \hline \end{array}$

1. Add. Use subtraction to check each answer.

   a)   4.157
          + 6.346   − _____

   b)   27.309
          + 14.167   − _____

   c)   3.187
          + 4.679   − _____

   d)   5.138
          + 12.349   − _____

   e)   0.573
          + 4.497   − _____

   f)   36.234
          + 14.875   − _____

2. Subtract. Use addition to check each answer.

   a)   7.243
          − 2.807   + _____

   b)   4.583
          − 2.338   + _____

   c)   13.040
          − 7.862   + _____

   d)   11.431
          − 8.763   + _____

   e)   4.010
          − 2.862   + _____

   f)   73.832
          − 51.765   + _____

3. The difference in the masses of 2 objects is 0.479 kg.

   a) What might the mass of each object be? _____

   b) What might the objects be? _____

4. Salvatore ran 2.457 km on Saturday and 3.169 km on Sunday.

   a) How far did Salvatore run in all? _____

   b) How much further did he run on Sunday than on Saturday?

   _____

Stretch Your Thinking . . . .

Use each of the digits 1 to 8 once
to make this subtraction true.

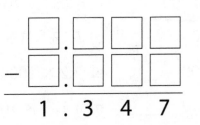

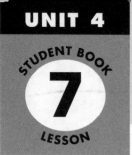
Multiplying Decimals by 10, 100, 1000, 10 000

Name

At Home
At School

Quick Review

Use mental math to multiply a decimal by 10, 100, 1000, and 10 000.

➤ When you multiply a decimal by 10, the digits shift 1 place to the left. You show this by moving the decimal point 1 place to the right.

$2.45 \times 10 = 24.5$
$0.432 \times 10 = 4.32$
$6.8 \times 10 = 68$

➤ When you multiply a decimal by 100, the digits shift 2 places to the left. You show this by moving the decimal point 2 places to the right.

$1.367 \times 100 = 136.7$
$5.3 \times 100 = 530$
$0.25 \times 100 = 25$

➤ When you multiply a decimal by 1000, the digits shift 3 places to the left. You show this by moving the decimal point 3 places to the right.

$5.846 \times 1000 = 5846$
$3.21 \times 1000 = 3210$
$0.004 \times 1000 = 4$

➤ When you multiply a decimal by 10 000, the digits shift 4 places to the left. You show this by moving the decimal point 4 places to the right.

$0.245 \times 10\,000 = 2450$
$1.26 \times 10\,000 = 12\,600$
$0.8 \times 10\,000 = 8000$

Try These

Use mental math to find each product.

1. **a)** $6.5 \times 10 =$ _____

$6.5 \times 100 =$ _____

$6.5 \times 1000 =$ _____

$6.5 \times 10\,000 =$ _____

b) $7.34 \times 10 =$ _____

$7.34 \times 100 =$ _____

$7.34 \times 1000 =$ _____

$7.34 \times 10\,000 =$ _____

c) $0.461 \times 10 =$ _____

$0.461 \times 100 =$ _____

$0.461 \times 1000 =$ _____

$0.461 \times 10\,000 =$ _____

2. **a)** $1.9 \times 10 =$ _____

b) $6.73 \times 100 =$ _____

c) $9.365 \times 10\,000 =$ _____

d) $2.6 \times 100 =$ _____

e) $7.2 \times 1000 =$ _____

f) $0.486 \times 1000 =$ _____

g) $2.63 \times 10 =$ _____

h) $1.123 \times 100 =$ _____

i) $0.586 \times 10\,000 =$ _____

Use mental math.

1. Use the information in the table to find the mass of each set of coins.

Masses of Coins	
Coin	**Mass (g)**
Penny	2.35
Nickel	3.95
Dime	1.75
Quarter	4.4
Toonie	7.3

   a) 10 000 quarters _____   b) 100 nickels _____

   c) 1000 dimes _____   d) 10 pennies _____

   e) 100 toonies _____   f) 1000 nickels _____

   g) 10 nickels _____   h) 10 000 dimes _____

2. Multiply.

   a) 5.03 × 10   b) 6.714 × 100   c) 0.415 × 1000   d) 62.3 × 10 000

   e) 62.345 × 1000   f) 8.173 × 10 000   g) 0.542 × 100   h) 3.7 × 1000

3. Write each distance in metres.

   a) 6.59 km _____   b) 0.927 km _____   c) 37.459 km _____

   d) 3.8 km _____   e) 5.47 km _____   f) 6.28 km _____

4. One bottle of spicy sauce has a capacity of 0.725 L. What is the capacity of 10 bottles? _____ 1000 bottles? _____ 10 000 bottles? _____

5. The width of a quarter is 23.88 mm. What is the distance covered by each number of quarters laid side by side?

   a) 10 _____   b) 100 _____   c) 10 000 _____

Stretch Your Thinking

1. Use the table in *Practice* question 1 to find the mass of:

   a) 101 pennies _____   b) 1001 nickels _____

   c) 11 quarters _____   d) 110 dimes _____

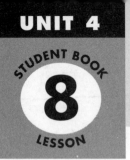
Dividing Decimals by 10, 100, 1000, 10 000

Name _____

Quick Review

At Home
At School

Use mental math to divide a decimal by 10, 100, 1000, and 10 000.

➤ When you divide a decimal by 10, the digits shift 1 place to the right. You show this by moving the decimal point 1 place to the left.

$3.62 \div 10 = 0.362$
$8.7 \div 10 = 0.87$
$6.8 \div 10 = 0.68$

➤ When you divide a decimal by 100, the digits shift 2 places to the right. You show this by moving the decimal point 2 places to the left.

$1.63 \div 100 = 0.0163$
$5.6 \div 100 = 0.056$
$3 \div 100 = 0.03$

➤ When you divide a decimal by 1000, the digits shift 3 places to the right. You show this by moving the decimal point 3 places to the left.

$4.415 \div 1000 = 0.004\ 15$
$7.2 \div 1000 = 0.0072$
$1 \div 1000 = 0.001$

➤ When you divide a decimal by 10 000, the digits shift 4 places to the right. You show this by moving the decimal point 4 places to the left.

$7.5 \div 10\ 000 = 0.000\ 75$
$1.4 \div 10\ 000 = 0.000\ 14$
$6 \div 10\ 000 = 0.0006$

Try These

Use mental math to find each quotient.

1. a) $8.2 \div 10 =$ _____

   $8.2 \div 100 =$ _____

   $8.2 \div 1000 =$ _____

   $8.2 \div 10\ 000 =$ _____

   b) $5 \div 10 =$ _____

   $5 \div 100 =$ _____

   $5 \div 1000 =$ _____

   $5 \div 10\ 000 =$ _____

2. a) $3.4 \div 10 =$ _____   b) $1.63 \div 100 =$ _____   c) $1.12 \div 1000 =$ _____

   d) $0.5 \div 100 =$ _____   e) $8 \div 10\ 000 =$ _____   f) $7 \div 10\ 000 =$ _____

   g) $5.17 \div 10 =$ _____   h) $9.6 \div 1000 =$ _____   i) $6.382 \div 10 =$ _____

Name _____

Use mental math.

1. **a)** $0.23 \div 10 =$ _____ **b)** $6 \div 10\,000 =$ _____

c) $78.3 \div 1000 =$ _____ **d)** $\$8.90 \div 10 =$ _____

e) $0.47 \div 1000 =$ _____ **f)** $2.146 \div 100 =$ _____

2. Write the missing divisor in each division sentence.

a) $4.23 \div$ _____ $= 0.0423$ **b)** $0.738 \div$ _____ $= 0.0738$

c) $5 \div$ _____ $= 0.05$ **d)** $3.2 \div$ _____ $= 0.000\,32$

e) $0.12 \div$ _____ $= 0.000\,12$ **f)** $173 \div$ _____ $= 0.0173$

3. A pile of 10 000 sheets of paper is 85 cm thick.

What is the thickness of 1 sheet of paper? _____

4. One hundred 50¢ coins have a mass of 690 g.

What is the mass of one 50¢ coin? _____

5. Jacob's scarf is 79 cm long.
Write this length in as many different units as you can.

_____

6. Sandy drank 575 mL of water during her walk.

Write this amount in litres. _____

7. Keshav jogged 1257 m today.
Write this distance in the units indicated.

_____ km; _____ cm; _____ dm; _____ mm

8. Helena's hair is 6.4 dm long. Write this length in metres. _____

9. One thousand seeds have a mass of 200 g.

What is the mass of 1 seed? _____

Stretch Your Thinking . . . .

One quarter has a mass of 4.4 g.
A bag of quarters has a mass of 2.64 kg.
What is the total value of the quarters? _____

Multiplying Whole Numbers by 0.1, 0.01, 0.001

Name _____

Quick Review

At Home
At School

Use mental math to multiply a whole number by 0.1, 0.01, and 0.001.
➤ When you multiply by 0.1, the digits shift 1 place to the right.
To show this, move the decimal point 1 place to the left.
$27 \times 0.1 = 2.7$
➤ When you multiply by 0.01, the digits shift 2 places to the right.
To show this, move the decimal point 2 places to the left.
$27 \times 0.01 = 0.27$
➤ When you multiply by 0.001, the digits shift 3 places to the right.
To show this, move the decimal point 3 places to the left.
$27 \times 0.001 = 0.027$

Try These •

Use mental math to multiply.

1. a) $2 \times 0.1 =$ _____   b) $74 \times 0.1 =$ _____   c) $235 \times 0.1 =$ _____

   $2 \times 0.01 =$ _____ $74 \times 0.01 =$ _____ $235 \times 0.01 =$ _____

   $2 \times 0.001 =$ _____ $74 \times 0.001 =$ _____ $235 \times 0.001 =$ _____

   d) $5 \times 0.1 =$ _____   e) $60 \times 0.1 =$ _____   f) $164 \times 0.1 =$ _____

   $5 \times 0.01 =$ _____ $60 \times 0.01 =$ _____ $164 \times 0.01 =$ _____

   $5 \times 0.001 =$ _____ $60 \times 0.001 =$ _____ $164 \times 0.001 =$ _____

2. a) $13 \times 0.1 =$ _____   b) $52 \times 0.001 =$ _____   c) $8 \times 0.01 =$ _____

   d) $59 \times 0.01 =$ _____   e) $3 \times 0.01 =$ _____   f) $231 \times 0.001 =$ _____

   g) $519 \times 0.001 =$ _____   h) $152 \times 0.1 =$ _____   i) $6 \times 0.001 =$ _____

   j) $7 \times 0.1 =$ _____   k) $6 \times 0.001 =$ _____   l) $73 \times 0.01 =$ _____

Use mental math to multiply.

1. a) $20 \times 0.01 =$ _____   **b)** $63 \times 0.001 =$ _____   **c)** $9 \times 0.1 =$ _____

d) $7 \times 0.001 =$ _____   **e)** $3 \times 0.01 =$ _____   **f)** $568 \times 0.01 =$ _____

g) $354 \times 0.1 =$ _____   **h)** $28 \times 0.1 =$ _____   **i)** $158 \times 0.001 =$ _____

2. Complete the table.

Number	× 0.1	× 0.01	× 0.001
39			
	4.7		
		1.52	
			0.098
194			

3. a) 75
$\times\ 0.1$

b) 1
$\times\ 0.001$

c) 71
$\times\ 0.01$

d) 13
$\times\ 0.1$

e) 9
$\times\ 0.01$

f) 154
$\times\ 0.01$

g) 62
$\times\ 0.001$

h) 486
$\times\ 0.1$

4. One jellybean has a mass of 0.001 kg. What is the mass of 98 jellybeans?

_____

A flower seed has a mass of 0.1 g.
What is the mass of 200 of these seeds? _____
How many seeds would it take to make 0.5 kg? _____

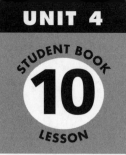
Multiplying Decimals by a 1-Digit Whole Number

At Home
At School

Quick Review

You can use what you know about multiplying whole numbers
to multiply a decimal by a whole number.
Multiply: 2.936×4

➤ First estimate.
Round 2.936 to 3.
$3 \times 4 = 12$
So 2.936×4 is about 12.

➤ Record the numbers without the
decimal point.
Multiply as you would with
whole numbers.

➤ Use the estimate to place the
decimal point in the product.
11.744 is close to 12, so
2.936×4 is 11.744.

```
        2936
      ×    4
          24
         120
        3600
        8000
      ───────
      11.744
```

Try These

Multiply.

1. a) 5.18
$\times\ 5$

b) 1.734
$\times\ 8$

c) 0.143
$\times\ 4$

d) 9.431
$\times\ 2$

Practice

1. Use paper and pencil to find each product.

   Record the products on the lines.

   Then use the letters next to the products to solve this riddle.

   Why did the jellybean go to school?

   0.396 × 5 = _____ (S)   1.637 × 3 = _____ (A)

   1.842 × 2 = _____ (X)   1.004 × 7 = _____ (T)

   0.176 × 4 = _____ (B)   8.145 × 6 = _____ (C)

   2.534 × 2 = _____ (D)   0.941 × 9 = _____ (W)

   1.935 × 4 = _____ (M)   2.123 × 4 = _____ (N)

   0.132 × 2 = _____ (E)   4.113 × 2 = _____ (R)

   3.005 × 3 = _____ (I)   1.254 × 3 = _____ (U)

   0.524 × 6 = _____ (H)   0.148 × 5 = _____ (O)

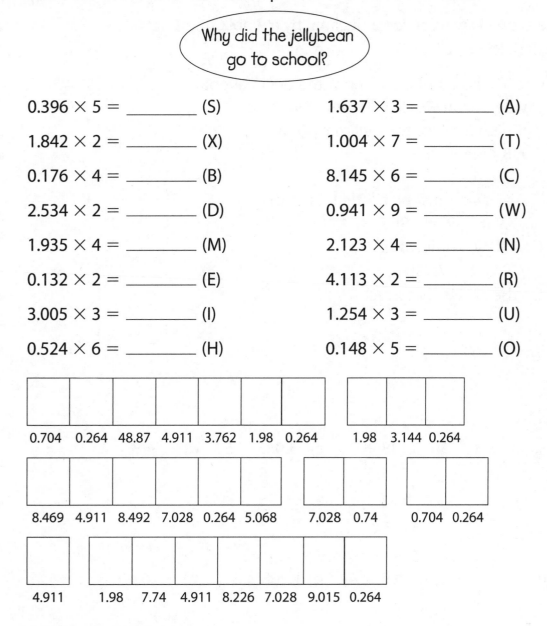

0.704 0.264 48.87 4.911 3.762 1.98 0.264   1.98 3.144 0.264

8.469 4.911 8.492 7.028 0.264 5.068   7.028 0.74   0.704 0.264

4.911   1.98 7.74 4.911 8.226 7.028 9.015 0.264

Stretch Your Thinking

What whole number would you multiply 6.374 by
to get the product 25.496? _____

63

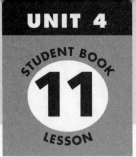
Dividing Decimals by a 1-Digit Whole Number

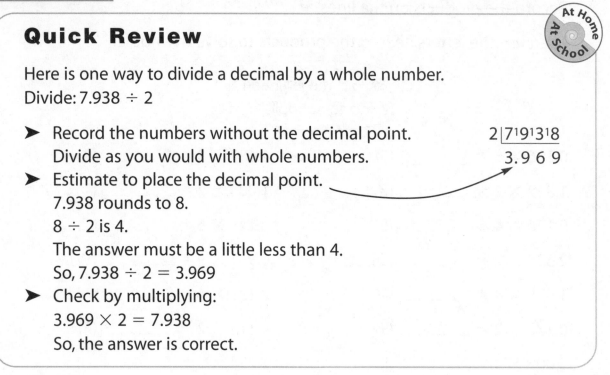

Quick Review

Here is one way to divide a decimal by a whole number.
Divide: $7.938 \div 2$

➤ Record the numbers without the decimal point.
Divide as you would with whole numbers.

$2\overline{)7\,^19\,^13\,^18}$
$3.9\ 6\ 9$

➤ Estimate to place the decimal point.
7.938 rounds to 8.
$8 \div 2$ is 4.
The answer must be a little less than 4.
So, $7.938 \div 2 = 3.969$
➤ Check by multiplying:
$3.969 \times 2 = 7.938$
So, the answer is correct.

Try These

1. Divide.

a) $3.896 \div 4$ b) $5.138 \div 2$ c) $3.045 \div 5$ d) $0.948 \div 2$

e) $0.924 \div 3$ f) $7.896 \div 4$ g) $1.268 \div 2$ h) $3.762 \div 6$

1. Divide.

    a) $5\overline{)5.335}$ **b)** $4\overline{)6.148}$ **c)** $7\overline{)0.315}$ **d)** $2\overline{)4.738}$

    e) $3\overline{)0.363}$ **f)** $8\overline{)1.144}$ **g)** $6\overline{)7.542}$ **h)** $8\overline{)17.072}$

2. Multiply to check each answer in question 1.

    a)   **b)**   **c)**   **d)**

    e)   **f)**   **g)**   **h)**

3. Renee paid $12.96 for 6 bags of chips.
How much did each bag cost? _____

4. Asmaa paid $9.96 for 3 pairs of socks.

Jagdeep paid $14.75 for 5 pairs of socks.

Which person got the better deal? Explain.

_____

_____

What whole number would you divide 2.049 by
to get the quotient 0.683? _____

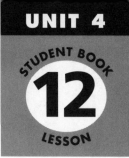

Dividing Decimals

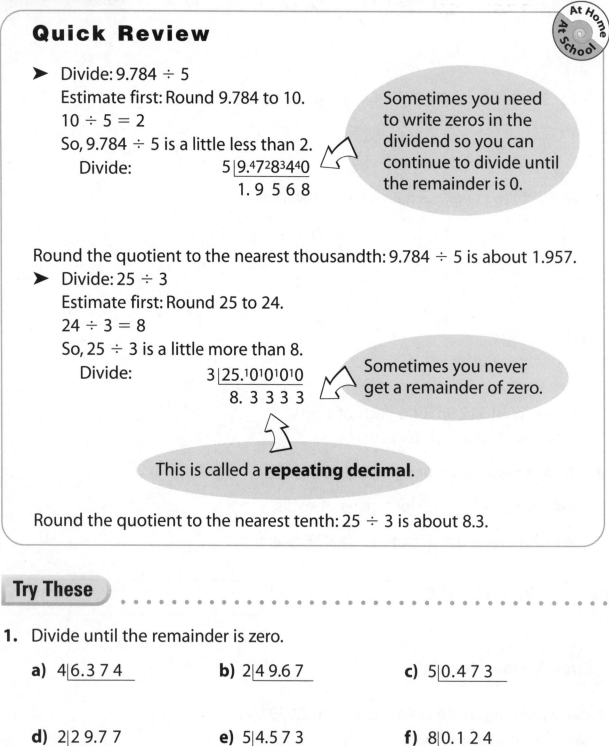

Quick Review

At Home
At School

➤ Divide: 9.784 ÷ 5
Estimate first: Round 9.784 to 10.
10 ÷ 5 = 2
So, 9.784 ÷ 5 is a little less than 2.

Divide: 5)9.$4^7$2^{8}3^{4}4^{4}0
          1. 9 5 6 8

Sometimes you need to write zeros in the dividend so you can continue to divide until the remainder is 0.

Round the quotient to the nearest thousandth: 9.784 ÷ 5 is about 1.957.

➤ Divide: 25 ÷ 3
Estimate first: Round 25 to 24.
24 ÷ 3 = 8
So, 25 ÷ 3 is a little more than 8.

Divide: 3)25.^{1}0^{1}0^{1}0^{1}0
          8. 3 3 3 3

Sometimes you never get a remainder of zero.

This is called a **repeating decimal**.

Round the quotient to the nearest tenth: 25 ÷ 3 is about 8.3.

Try These

1. Divide until the remainder is zero.

a) 4)6.3 7 4

b) 2)4 9.6 7

c) 5)0.4 7 3

d) 2)2 9.7 7

e) 5)4.5 7 3

f) 8)0.1 2 4

1. Divide until the remainder is zero.

   a) 6⌐4.2 7 5   **b)** 8⌐4 5   **c)** 5⌐2 3 4

   d) 2⌐0.0 0 7   **e)** 2⌐0.5   **f)** 4⌐2 7

2. Use a calculator to divide. Round each quotient to the nearest hundredth.

   a) 4 ÷ 11   **b)** 5 ÷ 8   **c)** 30 ÷ 11   **d)** 6 ÷ 7

   _____   _____   _____   _____

3. Four students buy a box of popsicles for $4.29 and a bag of pretzels for $3.97. How much should each person contribute to the total cost?

   _____

   _____

4. Nataliya jogged 1.367 km in 6 min.
   About how far did she jog each minute?
   Give your answer in as many different units as you can.

   _____

   _____

5. Twelve friends shared 8 small pizzas equally.
   How many pizzas did each person get?

   _____

1. **a)** Write a story problem you can solve by dividing 11 by 7.

   _____

   _____

   b) Solve your problem.

   _____

   _____

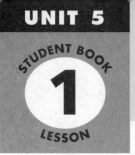
Interpreting Data

Name _____

Quick Review

This bar graph shows the average life spans of some Canadian animals. We **infer** that polar bears live about twice as long as beavers, and beavers about 3 times as long as raccoons.

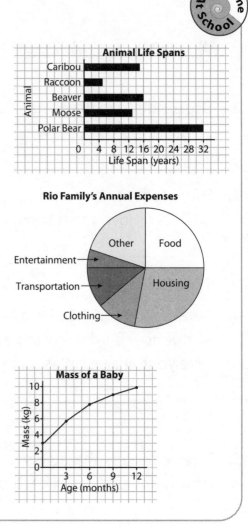

This circle graph shows the Rio family's annual expenses. We infer that food and housing make up about $\frac{1}{2}$ of the family's expenses.

This line graph shows the change in mass of a baby from birth to 12 months. We infer that the baby's mass increased steadily since birth.

Try These

1. What can you infer from this circle graph?

   _____

   _____

   _____

   _____

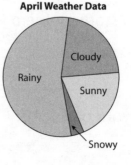

April Weather Data

1. Use the bar graph to answer these questions.

   a) Which river is about twice as long as the
      Fraser River? _____

   b) Which river is about one-third as long as the
      Mackenzie River? _____

   c) Which 2 rivers have a combined length of about
      4500 km? _____

2. What can you infer from each graph?

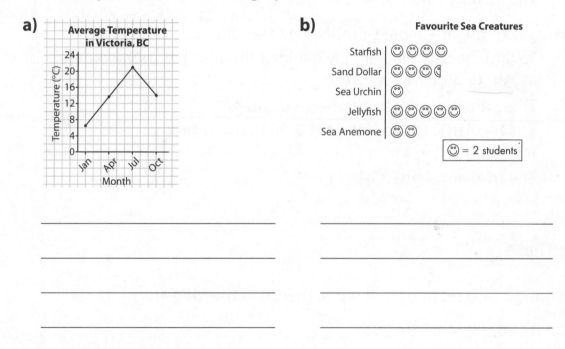

   a)

   _____

   _____

   _____

   _____

   b)

   _____

   _____

   _____

   _____

Stretch Your Thinking

What information can you determine from a bar graph that you cannot
determine from a circle graph?

_____

_____

_____

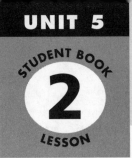

UNIT 5

STUDENT BOOK

2

LESSON

Finding the Median

Name

Quick Review

At Home At School

The **median** of a data set is the middle number when the data are arranged in order.

➤ Sayid caught 7 rainbow trout.
   He listed the lengths, in centimetres, from least to greatest:
   37, 39, 39, ⟨40⟩ 43, 44, 44
   The middle number is 40.
   The median length is 40 cm.

➤ Sayid caught 1 more trout, 42 cm in length.
   To find the new median, Sayid added this number to the ordered list:
   37, 39, 39, 40, 42, 43, 44, 44
   There are two middle numbers, 40 and 42.
   The median is the mean of the 2 middle numbers:
   (40 + 42) ÷ 2 = 41
   The median length is 41 cm.

Try These

1. Arrange each set of data in order. Then, find the median.

   a) 87, 76, 93, 74, 67, 91, 79 _____

   b) 12, 18, 27, 9, 42 _____

   c) 55, 45, 62, 71, 74, 58, 66, 58, 47 _____

   _____

   d) 17, 12, 18, 14, 16, 11 _____

   _____

   e) 44, 62, 17, 38, 59, 53, 48, 38 _____

   _____

70

1. Find the median of each set of data.

    a) $10, $14, $9, $11, $7, $12, $8 _____

    _____

    b) 305, 313, 342, 308, 324, 316 _____

    _____

2. **a)** Measure the arm spans and the strides of 5 people, to the nearest centimetre. Record your data in the table.

    b) What is the median arm span? _____

    Median stride? _____

    c) Measure one more person. What is the new median arm span?

    _____

    Median stride? _____

Name	Arm Span (cm)	Stride (cm)

3. This list shows the number of books 12 students read over the summer:

    8, 4, 13, 2, 4, 3, 5, 17, 7, 12, 4, 5

    a) Find these averages:

    mean _____   median _____   mode _____

    b) Which average best represents the number of books read? Why?

    _____

    _____

    _____

Stretch Your Thinking

Create a data set of 10 numbers with median 8 and mode 10.

_____

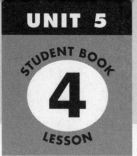

Constructing and Interpreting Graphs

Quick Review

At Home At School

This table shows the enrolment at Pearson School.

Year	1998	1999	2000	2001	2002	2003	2004
Enrolment	409	450	400	390	360	345	300

The data are given in categories. They can be shown in a bar graph.

The data show change over time. They can be shown in a line graph.

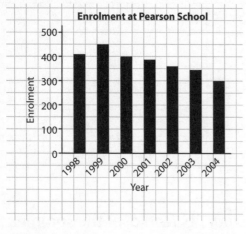

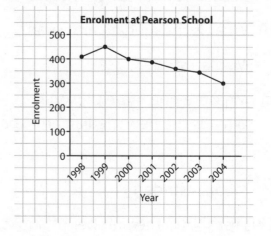

Both suggest an increase from 1998 to 1999, then a steady decrease.

Try These

1. a) Use the data in the table above. Redraw one graph using a different vertical scale.

   b) How does changing the vertical scale change the appearance of the data?

   _____

   _____

   _____

1. The table shows the value of Kundi's collection of hockey cards over time.

   a) Draw a line graph to display these data.

Kundi's Hockey Cards	
Year	Value ($)
2001	60
2002	80
2003	85
2004	100
2005	120

   b) What inferences can you make from your graph?

   _____

   _____

2. The table shows the annual number of foggy days at some airports.

   a) Draw a graph to display these data.

Airport	Number of Days
Vancouver	23
Calgary	21
Edmonton	10
Winnipeg	27
Toronto	16

   b) How did you choose the type of graph to use?

   _____

Stretch Your Thinking . . . .

Which type of graph would you use to display the monthly sales figures
for a bakery? Explain your choice.

_____

_____

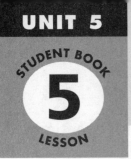
Graphing on a Coordinate Grid

Quick Review

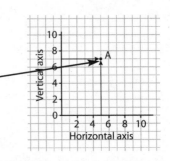

➤ We use an **ordered pair** to describe the coordinates of a point on a grid.

The coordinates of point A are (5, 7).

The **origin** is the point where the horizontal and vertical axes meet.
In an ordered pair:
• The first number tells the horizontal distance from the origin.
• The second number tells the vertical distance from the origin.

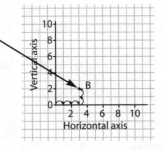

➤ The coordinates of point B are (3, 2).
To **plot** point B:
Start at the origin, move to 3 on the horizontal axis, then move up 2 units.

Try These

1. a) Name the letter on the grid represented by each ordered pair.

   (2, 5) ____   (6, 7) ____   (1, 4) ____

   (9, 6) ____   (7, 2) ____   (3, 8) ____

   b) Plot each point on the grid.

   G(5, 4), H(10, 10), I(0, 9),

   J(0, 2), K(8, 1), L(10, 4)

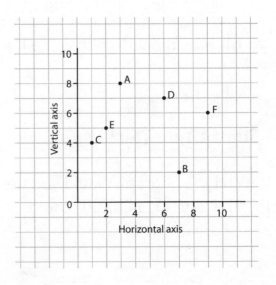

1. Plot each set of ordered pairs on the coordinate grid.
   Join the points in order.
   Join the last point to the first point.
   Name each polygon you have drawn.

   A: (8, 6), (6, 6), (6, 8), (8, 8)

   _____

   B: (0, 3), (4, 0), (6, 0), (2, 3)

   _____

   C: (1, 6), (1, 10), (4, 10), (4, 6)

   _____

   D: (7, 1), (6, 3), (8, 5), (10, 3), (9, 1)

   _____

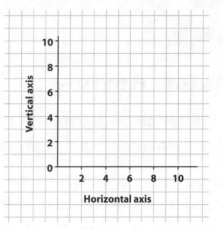

2. Plot six points on the grid.
   Label the points A to F.
   Record the ordered pairs.

   A: _____   B: _____

   C: _____   D: _____

   E: _____   F: _____

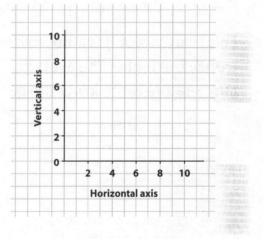

Stretch Your Thinking

(2, 5) and (7, 5) are 2 vertices of a
parallelogram with area 10 square units.
Plot the points for the 2 given vertices.
What are the coordinates of the other vertices?
Give as many answers as you can.

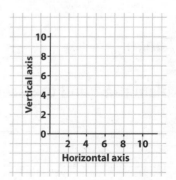

_____

_____

_____

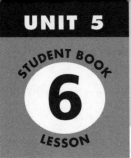
Scatter Plots

Name

Quick Review

A **scatter plot** is a graph of ordered pairs on a coordinate grid.
Each point on the grid represents two quantities.

This graph compares the time some students
spend on homework to their math scores.
Each point on the graph represents both
the time and the score for one student.

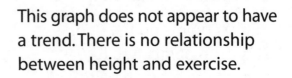

The graph has an **upward trend**.
The more time a student spends on homework, the better his or her score.

This scatter plot has a **downward trend**. The higher the average temperature is, the lower the gas bill.

This graph does not appear to have a trend. There is no relationship between height and exercise.

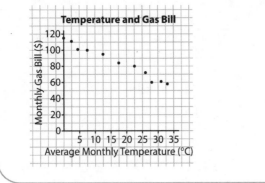

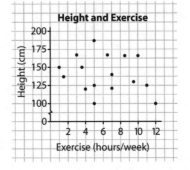

Try These

1. Explain the trend this scatter plot shows.

_____

_____

_____

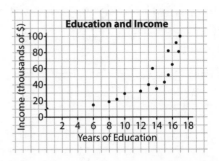

1. Describe the trend, if any, shown by each scatter plot.

a)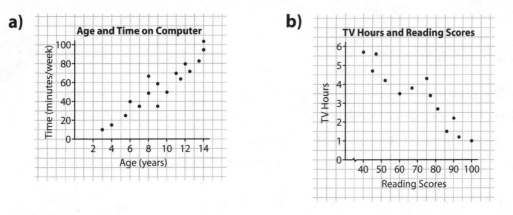

b)

_____   _____

_____   _____

2. This table shows the hand spans and hand lengths of some students.

Hand Length (cm)	12	10	13	13	12	15	17	15	16	16
Hand Span (cm)	14	13	14	16	16	18	20	17	14	20

   a) Draw a scatter plot of the data. In your math notebook

   b) Is there a trend in the graph? Explain.

   _____

   _____

   c) ~~Measure 4 more people.~~
      ~~Add these data to the scatter plot.~~
      ~~Do the data change the trend? Explain.~~

   _____

   _____

Stretch Your Thinking

What would you expect a scatter plot that compares length of hair to height

to look like? _____

_____

UNIT 5

STUDENT BOOK 7 LESSON

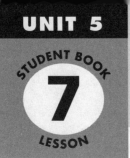

Conducting a Survey

Quick Review

When you write a survey question:
- ➤ The question should be understood by everyone the same way.
- ➤ All possible answers should be given.
- ➤ The question should not lead people to answer a certain way.

To ensure your results are not biased:
- ➤ Survey people who are typical of the population.
- ➤ If you cannot ask everyone in the population, ask as many people as you can.

The **population** is the entire group being discussed.

Lia surveyed all Grade 6 students in her school about their reading habits.

Here is her survey question:

How much time do you spend reading for pleasure each day?
- ☐ less than 15 min
- ☐ 15 to 30 min
- ☐ more than 30 min

Here are her results:

Time	Tally
less than 15 min	||
15 to 30 min	𝍸 𝍸 𝍸 𝍸 |||
more than 30 min	𝍸 𝍸

Try These

1. Display Lia's results in a bar graph.

2. What can you infer from the graph?

____

____

3. Do the results represent all Grade 6 students in Canada? Explain.

____

____

1. Write a survey question for each topic. List all possible answers.

   a) You want to find out the favourite amusement-park ride.

   _____

   _____

   b) You want to find out the least favourite vegetable.

   _____

   _____

   c) You want to investigate how people use computers.

   _____

   _____

2. Work with a partner. Write a survey question to find out about the parts of the newspaper your classmates read.
   Survey all the students in your class. Record your results in a table.

   _____

   _____

   _____

   _____

   _____

Stretch Your Thinking

How do you think your results for question 2 would change if you surveyed:

Adults? _____

_____

Teenagers? _____

_____

Time Zones

At Home
At School

Quick Review

You can use these maps of time zones to find the time in any place in Canada if you know the time in another place.

Winter Time Zones

Newfoundland Standard Time

Mountain Standard Time

Eastern Standard Time

Pacific Standard Time

Central Standard Time

Atlantic Standard Time

If it is 1:00 p.m. in the Pacific zone, it is 5:00 p.m. in the Atlantic zone.

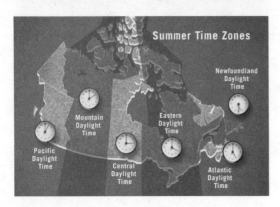

Summer Time Zones

Newfoundland Daylight Time

Mountain Daylight Time

Eastern Daylight Time

Pacific Daylight Time

Central Daylight Time

Atlantic Daylight Time

Daylight saving time lasts from the first Sunday in April until the last Sunday in October. Saskatchewan does not use daylight saving time.

Try These

Use the maps to help answer the questions.

1. In what time zone is the time 2 h ahead of:

   a) Pacific time?_____ **b)** Mountain time? _____

2. It is 7:00 a.m. in Toronto, ON. What time is it in:

   a) St. John's, NL? _____ **b)** Vancouver, BC? _____

   c) Winnipeg, MB? _____ **d)** Edmonton, AB? _____

Use the maps in the Quick Review.

1. It is 7:15 a.m. in Newfoundland. Is it earlier or later in Manitoba? _____

2. Suppose you are flying across Canada. You will have to set your watch to a later time when you land. In which direction are you flying? _____

3. It is 8:00 a.m. in Victoria, BC. What time is it in each city?

   a) Halifax, NS _____   b) Brandon, MB _____

   c) Ottawa, ON _____   d) Fredericton, NB _____

   e) Lethbridge, AB _____   f) Corner Brook, NL _____

   g) Montreal, QC _____   h) Prince George, BC _____

4. Sidra lives in Regina, SK. She phones her cousin in Charlottetown, PE, at 3:00 p.m. on May 5th.
   At what time does Sidra's cousin get the call? _____

5. What time will you arrive if you leave each place at the given time?

   a) Toronto, ON, at 3:00 p.m. for a 1-h flight to Montreal, QC _____

   b) Vancouver, BC, at 11:20 a.m. for a $4\frac{1}{2}$-h flight to Toronto, ON _____

   c) Winnipeg, MB, at 2:30 p.m. for a 2 h 5 min flight to Calgary, AB

   _____

6. Javier leaves Edmonton, AB, at 1:20 p.m. and arrives in St. John's, NL, at 8:45 p.m. How long is his flight? _____

7. Andrée lives in Prince Albert, SK. She got a phone call from her friend in Timmins, ON, at 4:30 p.m. on March 16.
   At what time did Andrée's friend make the call? _____

Stretch Your Thinking . . . .

Ask 4 classmates to each name a place in Canada he or she would like to visit in December. For each place, tell the time difference between it and where you live.

_____

_____

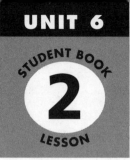
The 24-Hour Clock

Quick Review

This is a 24-h clock.
There are 24 h in one day.
From midnight to noon, the hours are from 0 to 12.
From 1 p.m. to midnight, the hours are from 13 to 24.

When we use the 24-h clock, we use 4 digits to write the time.

10:15 a.m. is written 10:15.	6:30 a.m. is written 06:30.	6:30 p.m. is written 18:30.

Here is how we write the time in seconds.

21:25:42 is 25 min and 42 s after 9 p.m.

Try These ·

1. Write each time in 24-h notation.

    a) 8:10 a.m. _____ **b)** 12:00 noon _____ **c)** 10:20 p.m. _____

2. Write each time in 12-h notation. Use a.m. or p.m.

    a) 06:12 _____ **b)** 10:55 _____ **c)** 13:43 _____

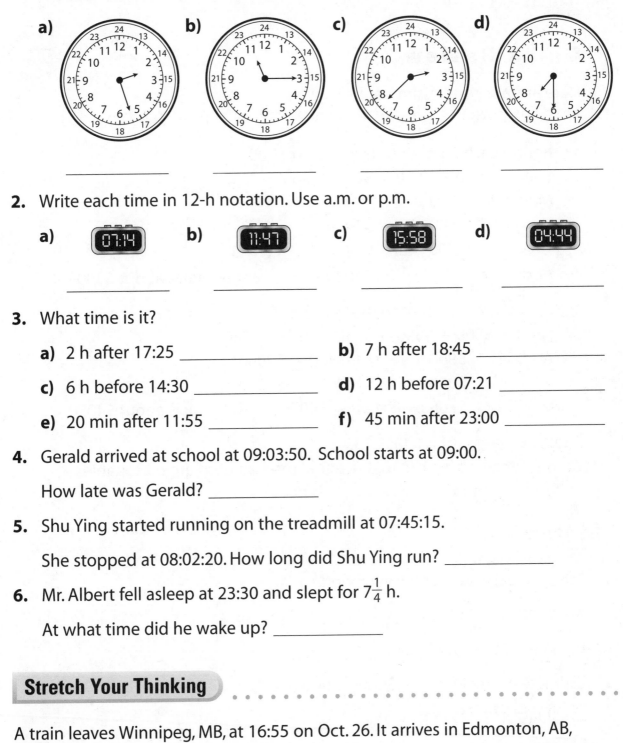

Practice

Name _____

1. Write each time in 24-h notation. Assume it is past noon.

   a) _____ b) _____ c) _____ d) _____

2. Write each time in 12-h notation. Use a.m. or p.m.

   a) `07:14` b) `11:47` c) `15:58` d) `04:44`

   _____ _____ _____ _____

3. What time is it?

   a) 2 h after 17:25 _____   b) 7 h after 18:45 _____

   c) 6 h before 14:30 _____   d) 12 h before 07:21 _____

   e) 20 min after 11:55 _____ f) 45 min after 23:00 _____

4. Gerald arrived at school at 09:03:50. School starts at 09:00.

   How late was Gerald? _____

5. Shu Ying started running on the treadmill at 07:45:15.

   She stopped at 08:02:20. How long did Shu Ying run? _____

6. Mr. Albert fell asleep at 23:30 and slept for $7\frac{1}{4}$ h.

   At what time did he wake up? _____

Stretch Your Thinking

A train leaves Winnipeg, MB, at 16:55 on Oct. 26. It arrives in Edmonton, AB,

at 08:05, Oct. 27. How long is the trip? _____

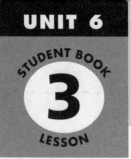

UNIT 6

STUDENT BOOK LESSON 3

Money to $10 000

Quick Review

At Home At School

Here are 2 ways to estimate the sum:
$818.69 + $784.18 + $553.78 + $843.25 + $641.83 + $409.40

➤ Round each amount to the nearest $100.
$800 + $800 + $600 + $800 + $600 + $400
Multiply: $800 × 3 = $2400
           $600 × 2 = $1200
           $400 × 1 = $ 400
                      ‾‾‾‾‾‾
Add: $4000   The total is about $4000.

➤ Round each amount to the nearest $50.
$800 + $800 + $550 + $850 + $650 + $400
Add: $800 + $800 + $400 = $2000
          $850 + $550 + $650 = $2050
          $2000 + $2050 = $4050   The total is about $4050.

The actual amount is $4051.13.
Both estimates are close to the actual total, so both are reasonable.

Try These

1. Estimate each sum. Show your work.

   a) $729.45 + $378.71 _____

   b) $1341.75 + $7605.19 _____

2. Estimate each difference. Show your work.

   a) $5867.43 − $2111.15 _____

   b) $967.41 − $386.91 _____

3. Write each amount in numbers.

   a) two hundred forty-six dollars _____   **b)** four thousand one dollars _____

84

1. Estimate each sum or difference. Show your work.

   a) $763.24 + $524.91 + $328.14 + $694.25

   _____

   b) $2184.16 + $4876.84 + $1414.33

   _____

   c) $9967.73 − $4361.20

   _____

2. Work with a partner.
   Take turns to choose an item from
   a catalogue or flyer.
   The price of each item is to be
   between $500 and $1000.
   Record your data in the table.
   Stop when you estimate your total
   is close to, but not greater than, $4000.
   Use a calculator to find the actual total.

Item	Price
Estimated Total:	
Actual Total:	

3. Murti bought a plasma TV for $2784.95 and a video recorder for $826.35.
   About how much did Murti spend? _____

Stretch Your Thinking

Before her trip to Hong Kong, Oga exchanged C$500 for HK$3287. About how
many Hong Kong dollars did Oga receive for each Canadian dollar?

_____

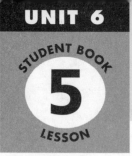
Surface Area of a Rectangular Prism

At Home
At School

Quick Review

The **surface area** of an object is the sum of the areas of its faces.
Here is a rectangular prism and its net.
To find the area of the prism, find the areas of its faces, then add.

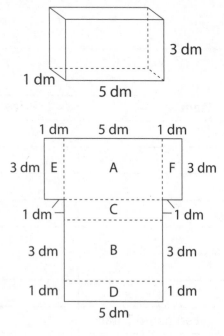

Face	Length (dm)	Width (dm)	Area (dm²)
A	5	3	15
B	5	3	15
C	5	1	5
D	5	1	5
E	1	3	3
F	1	3	3
		Total	46

The surface area of the prism is 46 dm².

Try These

1. Sketch a net of this rectangular prism. Find its surface area.

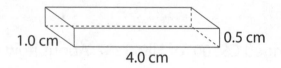

Surface area = _____

86

Name

1. Find the surface area of each rectangular prism.

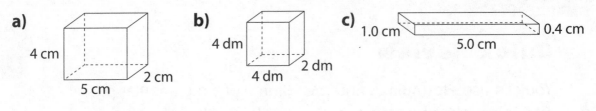

a)

4 cm
5 cm
2 cm

b)

4 dm
4 dm
2 dm

c)

1.0 cm
5.0 cm
0.4 cm

_____   _____   _____

2. Two blocks of cheese have approximately the same mass. One measures
   7 cm × 6 cm × 12 cm and the other measures 8 cm × 8 cm × 8 cm.
   Which block will need more shrink wrap? Explain.

   _____

   _____

3. a) Find 3 small boxes that have the shape of a rectangular prism.
      Label the boxes A, B, and C. Predict the order of the boxes from
      least to greatest surface area. _____

   b) Sketch the 3 boxes. Measure and label their dimensions.
      Find the surface area of each box.

            Box A   Box B   Box C

      _____   _____   _____

   c) Order the boxes from least to greatest surface area. _____

Find the surface area of a number cube with side measure 1.5 cm. _____

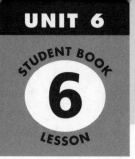

UNIT 6
STUDENT BOOK 6 LESSON

Volume of a Rectangular Prism

Quick Review

You can use a formula to find the volume of a rectangular prism.
The volume is the product of the prism's length, width, and height.

Volume = Length × Width × Height

This rectangular prism is 7.0 cm long,
3.5 cm wide, and 2.3 cm high.
Volume = 7.0 cm × 3.5 cm × 2.3 cm
        = 24.5 cm² × 2.3 cm
        = 56.35 cm³

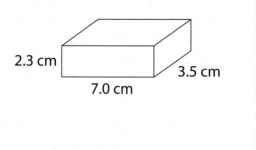

2.3 cm
3.5 cm
7.0 cm

The volume of the prism is 56.35 cm³.

Try These

1. Find the volume of each rectangular prism.

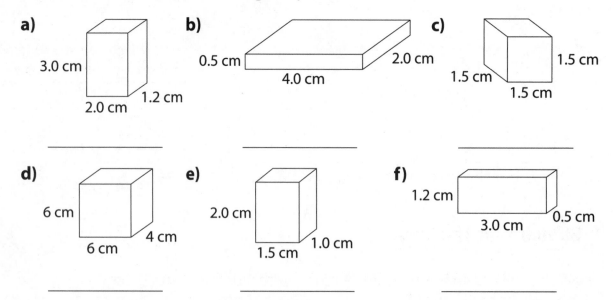

a)
3.0 cm
2.0 cm
1.2 cm

b)
0.5 cm
4.0 cm
2.0 cm

c)
1.5 cm
1.5 cm
1.5 cm

d)
6 cm
6 cm
4 cm

e)
2.0 cm
1.5 cm
1.0 cm

f)
1.2 cm
3.0 cm
0.5 cm

1. Find the volume of each aquarium.

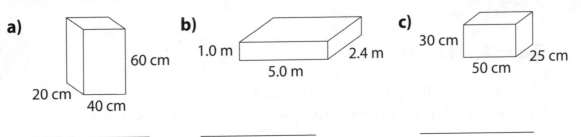

a)   60 cm   20 cm   40 cm

b)   1.0 m   5.0 m   2.4 m

c)   30 cm   50 cm   25 cm

_____   _____   _____

2. Work with a partner.

   a) Find 4 small boxes. Label the boxes A, B, C, and D.

   b) Measure the dimensions of each box. Estimate, then calculate, each volume. Record your results in the table.

Box	Length	Width	Height	Estimated Volume	Actual Volume
A					
B					
C					
D					

3. Complete each table.

a)

Length (cm)	Width (cm)	Height (cm)	Volume (cm³)
6	9	3	
8		2	80
4	3		48
	5	5	125

b)

Length (cm)	Width (cm)	Height (cm)	Volume (cm³)
5.3	4.0	7.1	
6.0	3.2		96
	2.0	1.1	22
12.0		4.0	120

Stretch Your Thinking . . . .

Jocelyn built a rectangular prism with 36 centimetre cubes.
What might be the dimensions of the prism? Give as many answers as you can.

_____

_____

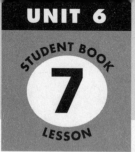
The Cubic Metre

Quick Review

A line segment has only one dimension.
It is measured using **linear units** such as centimetres and metres.

A flat surface has two dimensions.
The area it covers is measured using **square units** such as square centimetres or square metres.

An object has three dimensions.
The space it occupies is measured using **cubic units** such as cubic centimetres or cubic metres.

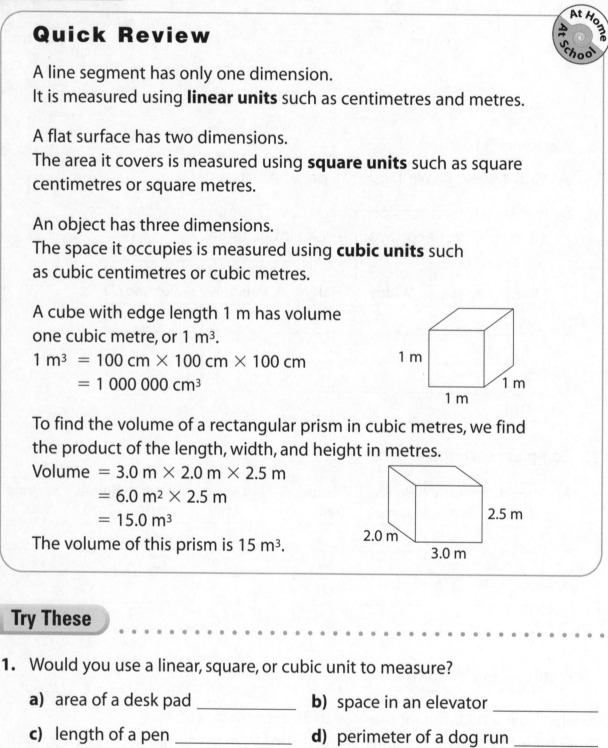

A cube with edge length 1 m has volume one cubic metre, or 1 m^3.
$1 \text{ m}^3 = 100 \text{ cm} \times 100 \text{ cm} \times 100 \text{ cm}$
$\qquad = 1\,000\,000 \text{ cm}^3$

To find the volume of a rectangular prism in cubic metres, we find the product of the length, width, and height in metres.

Volume $= 3.0 \text{ m} \times 2.0 \text{ m} \times 2.5 \text{ m}$
$\qquad = 6.0 \text{ m}^2 \times 2.5 \text{ m}$
$\qquad = 15.0 \text{ m}^3$
The volume of this prism is 15 m^3.

Try These

1. Would you use a linear, square, or cubic unit to measure?

   a) area of a desk pad _____   **b)** space in an elevator _____

   c) length of a pen _____   **d)** perimeter of a dog run _____

Practice

1. Find the volume of each box in cubic metres.

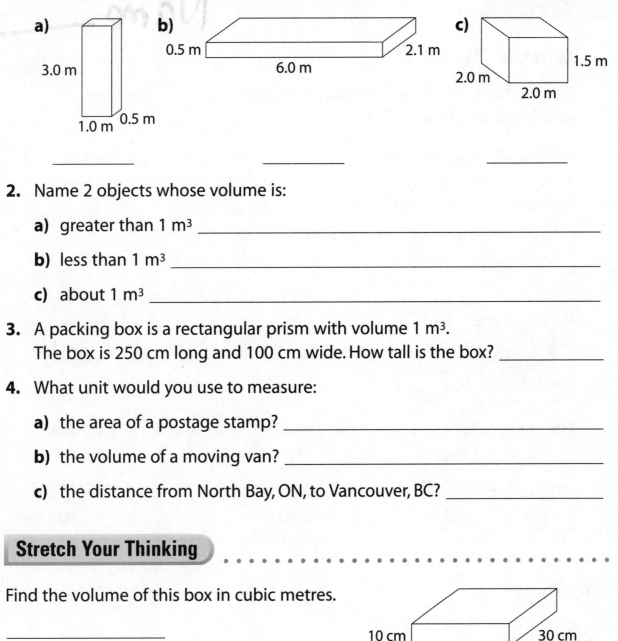

   a) 3.0 m, 1.0 m, 0.5 m

   b) 0.5 m, 6.0 m, 2.1 m

   c) 2.0 m, 2.0 m, 1.5 m

   _____   _____   _____

2. Name 2 objects whose volume is:

   a) greater than 1 m³ _____

   b) less than 1 m³ _____

   c) about 1 m³ _____

3. A packing box is a rectangular prism with volume 1 m³.
   The box is 250 cm long and 100 cm wide. How tall is the box? _____

4. What unit would you use to measure:

   a) the area of a postage stamp? _____

   b) the volume of a moving van? _____

   c) the distance from North Bay, ON, to Vancouver, BC? _____

Stretch Your Thinking

Find the volume of this box in cubic metres.

_____   10 cm   30 cm   45 cm

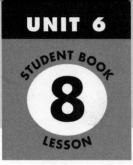

Capacity and Volume

Name

Quick Review

Units of both volume and capacity are used to measure the "size" of three-dimensional objects.

Units of capacity are used to measure liquids or gases and the containers that hold them.

Units of volume are used to measure the space an object occupies.

Use these relationships to convert between units of volume and capacity:

$$1 \text{ cm}^3 = 1 \text{ mL} \qquad 1 \text{ m}^3 = 1000 \text{ L} \qquad 1000 \text{ cm}^3 = 1 \text{ L}$$

$$255 \text{ cm}^3 = \frac{255}{1000} \text{ L} \qquad 6.7 \text{ m}^3 = 6.7 \times 1000 \text{ L} \qquad 724 \text{ L} = \frac{724}{1000} \text{ m}^3$$
$$= 0.255 \text{ L} \qquad = 6700 \text{ L} \qquad = 0.724 \text{ m}^3$$

Try These

1. Complete.

   a) 1750 mL = _____ L

   b) 7 m³ = _____ cm³

   c) 200 000 cm³ = _____ m³

   d) 6 m³ = _____ L

   e) 75 mL = _____ cm³

   f) 317 cm³ = _____ L

   g) 94 cm³ = _____ mL

   h) 4.2 L = _____ cm³

2. How many litres of water would it take to fill a swimming pool 9 m long, 5 m wide, and 2 m deep? _____

1. Circle the best estimate of volume or capacity.

   a) a barrel of water   75 mL   180 L   150 m³

   b) a bowl of porridge   20 L   400 mL   35 cm³

   c) a moving van   135 m³   4 m³   75 L

2. Selena's rectangular swimming pool holds 36 000 L of water.

   a) Find the volume of water in cubic metres. _____

   b) The pool is 2 m deep. How long and how wide might it be?

   _____

3. Find the volume of water, in litres, needed to fill each fish tank.

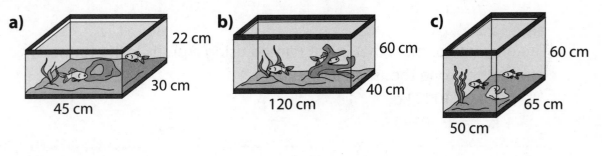

   a) 22 cm, 30 cm, 45 cm

   b) 60 cm, 40 cm, 120 cm

   c) 60 cm, 65 cm, 50 cm

   _____   _____   _____

4. Look at a milk carton.
   How much milk does it contain in litres? _____ In millilitres? _____

   Write this amount in cubic centimetres. _____

5. Describe how you might find the volume of a golf ball.

   _____

   _____

   _____

Stretch Your Thinking . . . .

One kilolitre is equal to 1000 L.
How many kilolitres of water would it take to fill a pool 9 m × 6 m × 2 m?

_____

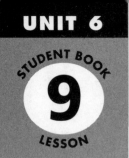

Relating Units of Mass

Quick Review

At Home At School

The gram is the basic unit of mass in the metric system.
The other units are named by adding prefixes to the word "gram."

The prefix "milli"
means thousandths.
So, one milligram is
one-thousandth of a gram.

$1 \text{ mg} = 0.001 \text{ g}$
$1000 \text{ mg} = 1000 \times 0.001 \text{ g}$
$= 1 \text{ g}$

The prefix "kilo"
means thousands.
So, one kilogram is
one thousand grams.

$1 \text{ kg} = 1000 \text{ g}$
$1 \text{ g} = 0.001 \text{ kg}$

The only unit of mass that is not named using a prefix is the tonne.
One tonne is one thousand kilograms.

$1 \text{ t} = 1000 \text{ kg}$
$1 \text{ kg} = 0.001 \text{ t}$

Try These

1. Which unit would you use to measure the mass of:

   a seed? _____ a fruit bar? _____ an elephant? _____

2. Write each mass using 2 different units.

   a) 225 g _____   **b)** 1.6 t _____

   c) 1367 g _____   **d)** 5 kg _____

3. Which package contains more cereal,
   A or B? _____

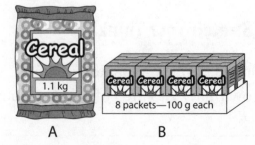

Cereal
1.1 kg

Cereal Cereal Cereal Cereal
8 packets—100 g each

A   B

Name

1. Complete.

a) 300 g = _____ mg b) 2370 mg = _____ g c) 0.4 g = _____ mg

d) 2 g = _____ mg e) 75 mg = _____ g f) 40 mg = _____ g

g) 2580 mg = _____ g h) 55 g = _____ mg i) 3.7 g = _____ mg

2. Complete.

a) 45 kg = _____ g b) 109 g = _____ kg c) 6178 g = _____ kg

d) 1.31 kg = _____ g e) 6273 kg = _____ t f) 2.63 t = _____ kg

g) 41 317 kg = _____ t h) 19.72 t = _____ kg i) 0.14 kg = _____ g

3. A farmer sold 2.6 t of apples to a juice company for $2600.

   How much did the farmer receive per kilogram? _____

4. About how many grams of dog food are in a pouch?

   _____

5. A banana has a mass of about 200 g. How many bananas could be in 4 kg?

   _____

6. Apples cost $2.20 per kilogram. Hiti needs 750 g of apples to put in a fruit

   salad. How much will she pay for the apples? _____

7. A large bus has a mass of about 12 200 kg.

   Write its mass using 2 different units. _____

Which brand of spaghetti is the best buy?
Explain.

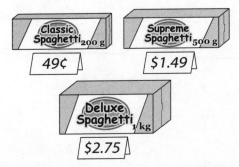

_____

_____

_____

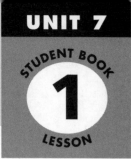
Transformations

Quick Review

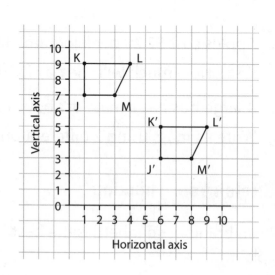
At Home
At School

We can show transformations on a coordinate grid.

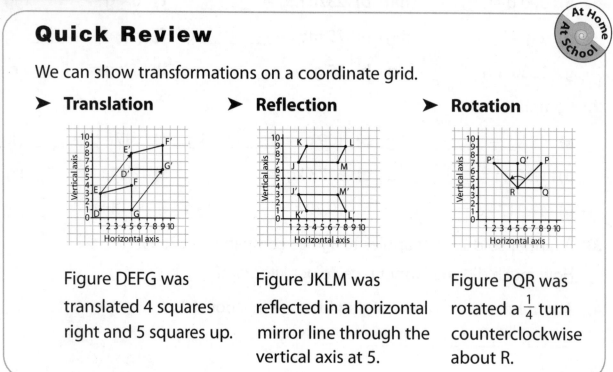

➤ **Translation**

➤ **Reflection**

➤ **Rotation**

Figure DEFG was translated 4 squares right and 5 squares up.

Figure JKLM was reflected in a horizontal mirror line through the vertical axis at 5.

Figure PQR was rotated a $\frac{1}{4}$ turn counterclockwise about R.

Try These

1. **a)** Identify this transformation.

   _____

   _____

   b) Write the coordinates of the vertices of the figure and its image.

   _____

   _____

Practice

1. Describe as many different transformations as you can that would move Figure EFGH onto the image.

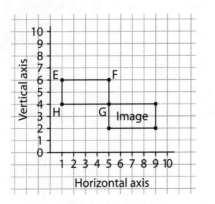

_____

_____

2. **a)** Draw the image of Figure JKLM after a $\frac{1}{4}$ turn clockwise about L. Label the vertices of the image.

   b) Write the coordinates of the figure.

   _____

   c) Write the coordinates of the image.

   _____

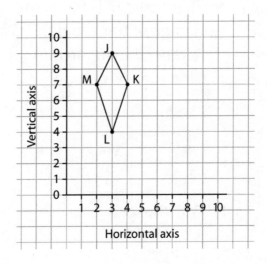

Stretch Your Thinking

Draw a figure for which a translation image could also be a reflection image. Draw the image. Write the coordinates of the figure and the image.

_____

_____

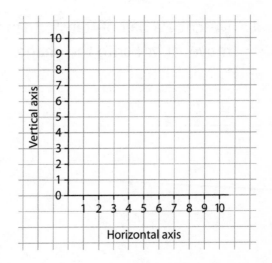

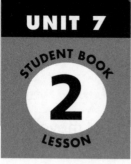
Combined Transformations

Quick Review

At Home At School

➤ Triangle ABC has been translated 5 squares right and 2 squares down, and then reflected in a horizontal line through 4 on the vertical axis.

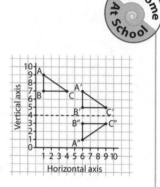

➤ Trapezoid D″E″FG″ is the image of trapezoid DEFG after a reflection in the mirror line, and then a rotation.

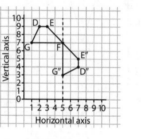

To identify the reflection, work backward.
D′E′FG′ is the reflection image of trapezoid DEFG.

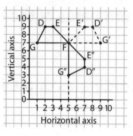

Try These

1. Describe a pair of transformations that move △LMN onto the image.

_____

_____

_____

_____

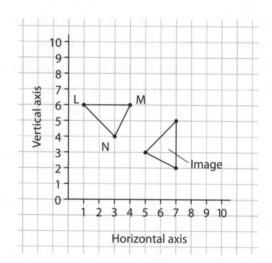

1. **a)** Translate △QRS 3 squares right and 2 squares down.
   Then reflect the translation image in a vertical line through 7 on the horizontal axis.

   b) List the coordinates of the final image.

   _____

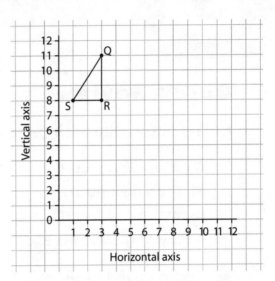

2. **a)** Draw a figure whose vertices have these coordinates:

   A(4, 10)   B(7, 10)   C(8, 8)

   D(6, 6)   E(3, 8)

   b) Rotate the figure 180° about D. Draw the rotation figure and label its vertices.

   c) List the coordinates of the final image.

   _____

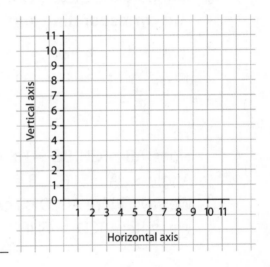

Stretch Your Thinking

Apply transformations to the triangle to make a design. Explain how you did it.

_____

_____

_____

_____

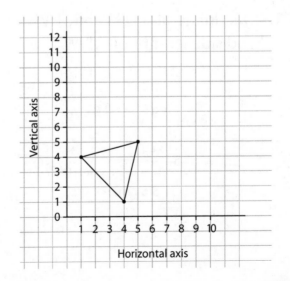

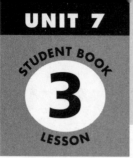

UNIT 7

STUDENT BOOK 3 LESSON

Congruent Figures

Quick Review

Here is one way to tell if these figures are congruent.

➤ Measure and record all the side lengths.
Measure and record all the angle measures.

➤ Compare the measures of **corresponding sides** and **corresponding angles**.

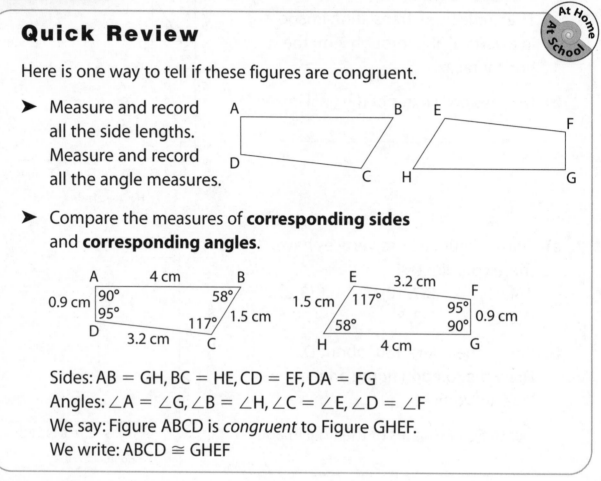

Sides: AB = GH, BC = HE, CD = EF, DA = FG
Angles: $\angle A = \angle G$, $\angle B = \angle H$, $\angle C = \angle E$, $\angle D = \angle F$
We say: Figure ABCD is *congruent* to Figure GHEF.
We write: ABCD $\cong$ GHEF

Try These

1. Quadrilaterals PQRS and TUVW are congruent. Label the angle measures and side lengths of TUVW.

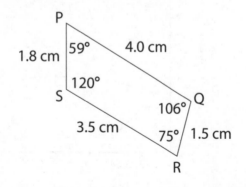

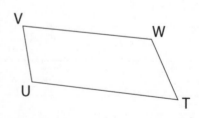

1. Draw a pentagon. Label the vertices ABCDE. Then draw a pentagon that is congruent to ABCDE. Label it JKLMN.

2. Which of these polygons are congruent? Explain how you know.

_____

_____

_____

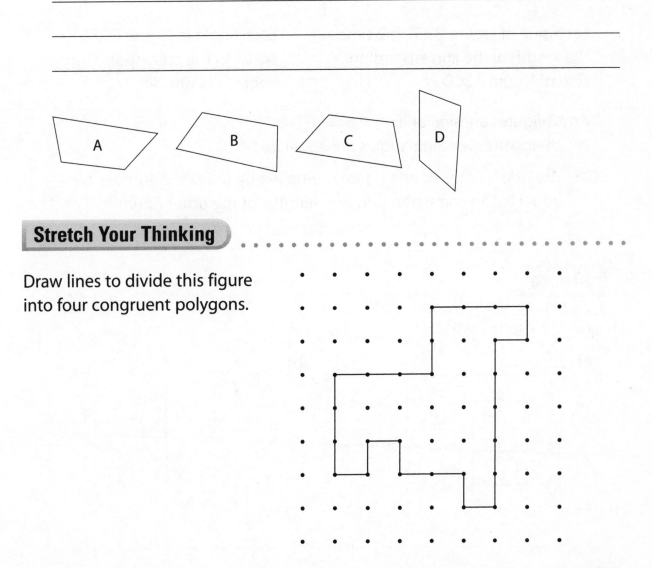

Stretch Your Thinking . . . .

Draw lines to divide this figure into four congruent polygons.

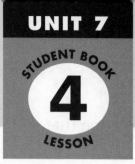
Similar Figures

Quick Review

At Home
At School

These figures are similar.

We say: ABCD is similar to QRST.
We write: ABCD ~ QRST

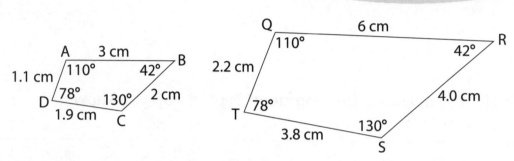

Each side of Figure QRST is 2 times the length of the corresponding side of Figure ABCD.

Each angle in Figure QRST is equal to the corresponding angle in Figure ABCD.

Any 2 figures are similar if:

➤ their corresponding angles are equal *and*

➤ the side lengths of one figure multiplied by the same number are equal to the corresponding side lengths of the other figure

Try These

1. Are the figures similar?

   a)

   b)

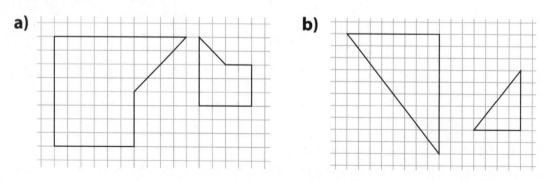

1. Are the figures similar?

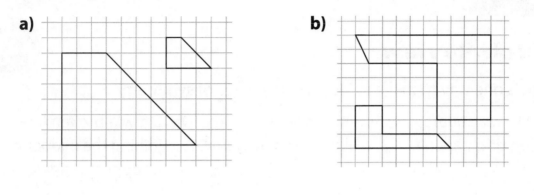

a) _____   b) _____

2. Find a pair of similar figures. Label each figure with an A. Continue to find pairs of similar figures. Label each pair with a different letter.

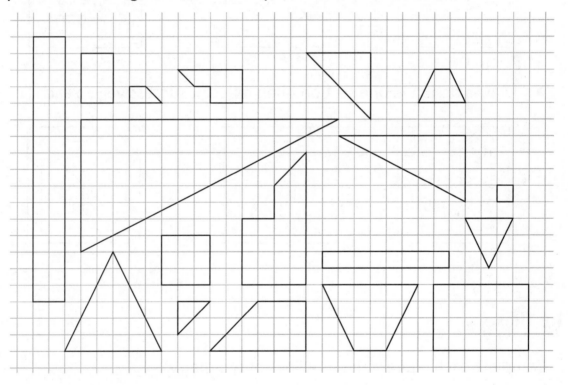

Stretch Your Thinking

A rectangle measures 5 m by 8 m.

A similar rectangle has a side measurement of 40 m.

What is the other side measurement of the larger rectangle?

Find two possible answers. _____

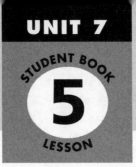

Line Symmetry

Quick Review

Here is one way to make a design with 4 lines of symmetry.

➤ Draw a square on grid paper.

➤ Draw a broken line along each diagonal.

➤ Draw a broken line joining the midpoints of opposite sides.

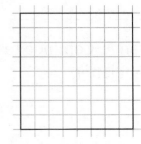 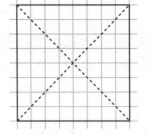 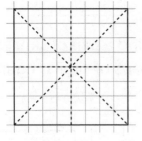

➤ Draw a design in one section. Then reflect it successively in each line.

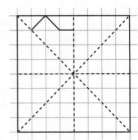 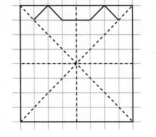 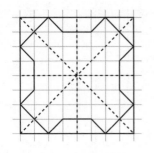

Try These

1. Complete each figure so it has 4 lines of symmetry.

a)

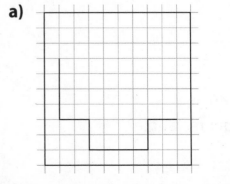

b)

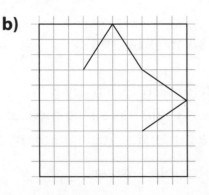

104

1. Draw a design in one section of the square. Reflect the design in the broken lines to complete the picture.

2. Draw 3 different polygons that have only 2 lines of symmetry. Show the lines of symmetry.

Identify the lines of symmetry in this design.

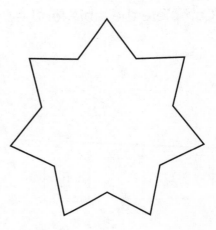

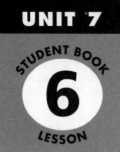
Rotational Symmetry

At Home
At School

Quick Review

A figure that coincides with itself when rotated less than a full turn
has **rotational symmetry**.

➤ This figure coincides with itself 2 times in one full turn.
  It has rotational symmetry of order 2.

➤ This figure does not coincide with itself in less than a full turn.
  It has no rotational symmetry.

Try These

1. Complete the table for the polygons.

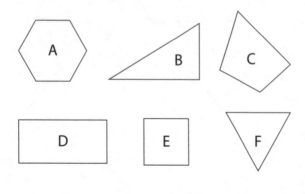

Polygon	Does It Have Rotational Symmetry?	Order of Rotational Symmetry
A		
B		
C		
D		
E		
F		

1. For each polygon, find the order of rotational symmetry.

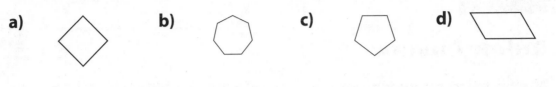

   a)   b)   c)   d)

   _____   _____   _____   _____

2. Add more squares to each figure so that it has rotational symmetry of order 2.

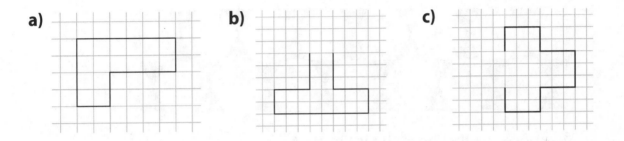

   a)   b)   c)

3. Draw a figure with each order of rotational symmetry.

   a) order 3   b) order 2   c) order 6

   . . . .

   . . . .

   . . . .

   . . . .

   . . . .

Stretch Your Thinking . . . .

Which of these letters have rotational symmetry?

_____

N M Z H
A I O E

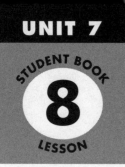
Tiling Patterns

Quick Review

A tiling pattern covers a surface with no gaps or overlaps.

This tiling pattern is made with congruent copies of a regular hexagon and an equilateral triangle.

Suppose the first hexagon is Figure A.
To get Figure B, rotate Figure A about the vertex it shares with Figure B.
Continue to rotate to make the design.
You could also make the design by reflecting or translating.

Try These

1. Explain how you could use transformations to make this pattern.

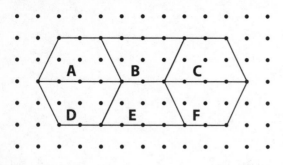

_____

_____

_____

_____

1. Add one row of figures to each tiling pattern.

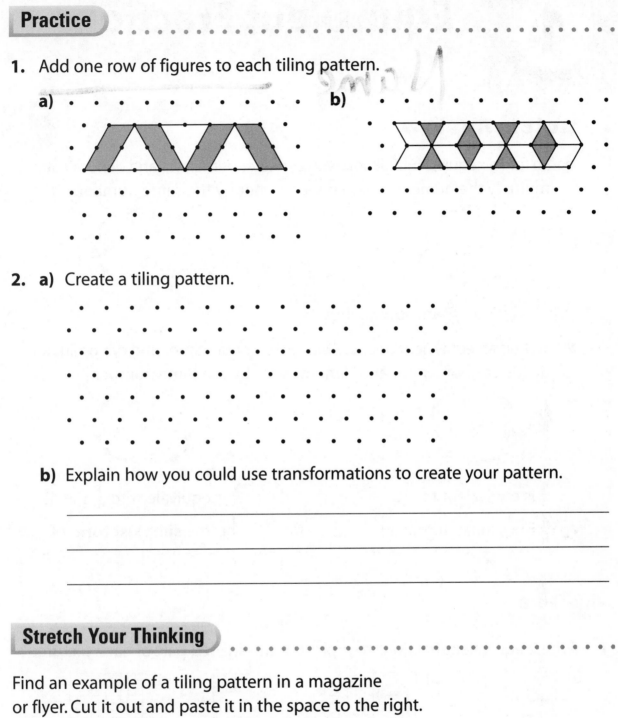

a)

b)

2. a) Create a tiling pattern.

   b) Explain how you could use transformations to create your pattern.

   _____

   _____

   _____

Stretch Your Thinking

Find an example of a tiling pattern in a magazine
or flyer. Cut it out and paste it in the space to the right.
Explain how transformations could have been used
to create the pattern.

_____

_____

_____

Equivalent Fractions

Name _____

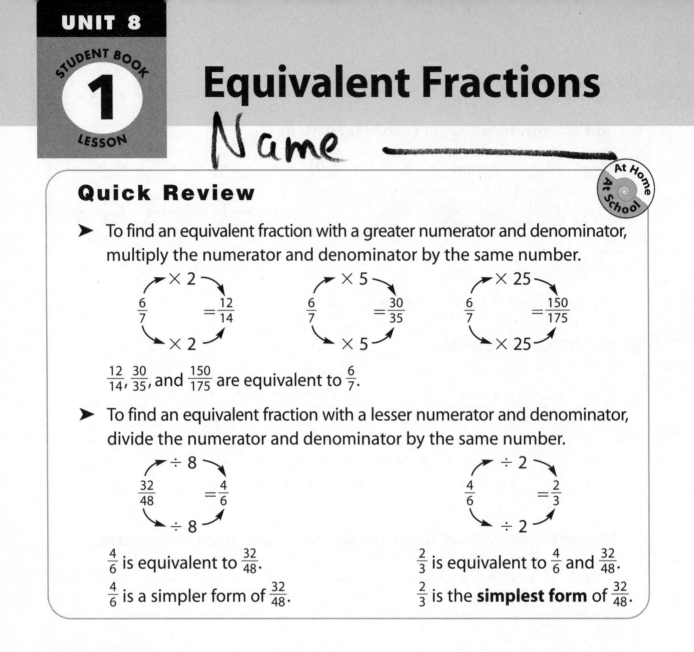

Quick Review

➤ To find an equivalent fraction with a greater numerator and denominator, multiply the numerator and denominator by the same number.

$$\frac{6}{7} \overset{\times 2}{=} \frac{12}{14} \qquad \frac{6}{7} \overset{\times 5}{=} \frac{30}{35} \qquad \frac{6}{7} \overset{\times 25}{=} \frac{150}{175}$$

$\frac{12}{14}, \frac{30}{35},$ and $\frac{150}{175}$ are equivalent to $\frac{6}{7}$.

➤ To find an equivalent fraction with a lesser numerator and denominator, divide the numerator and denominator by the same number.

$$\frac{32}{48} \overset{\div 8}{=} \frac{4}{6} \qquad\qquad \frac{4}{6} \overset{\div 2}{=} \frac{2}{3}$$

$\frac{4}{6}$ is equivalent to $\frac{32}{48}$.

$\frac{4}{6}$ is a simpler form of $\frac{32}{48}$.

$\frac{2}{3}$ is equivalent to $\frac{4}{6}$ and $\frac{32}{48}$.

$\frac{2}{3}$ is the **simplest form** of $\frac{32}{48}$.

Try These

1. Write 2 equivalent fractions to represent the shaded part of each picture.

a)   b)   c)   d)

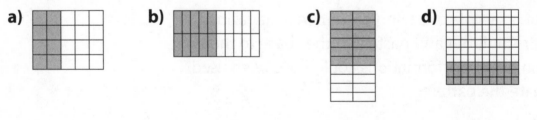

____ ____   ____ ____   ____ ____   ____ ____

2. Write 2 equivalent fractions to represent the unshaded part of each picture in question 1.

a) ____ ____   b) ____ ____   c) ____ ____   d) ____ ____

1. Multiply to find an equivalent fraction.

   a) $\frac{5}{6}$ = ____   b) $\frac{7}{12}$ = ____   c) $\frac{4}{9}$ = ____   d) $\frac{3}{8}$ = ____

   e) $\frac{6}{7}$ = ____   f) $\frac{2}{3}$ = ____   g) $\frac{3}{11}$ = ____   h) $\frac{17}{25}$ = ____

2. Divide to find an equivalent fraction.

   a) $\frac{18}{24}$ = ____   b) $\frac{30}{36}$ = ____   c) $\frac{125}{175}$ = ____   d) $\frac{18}{81}$ = ____

   e) $\frac{21}{49}$ = ____   f) $\frac{80}{100}$ = ____   g) $\frac{500}{900}$ = ____   h) $\frac{30}{54}$ = ____

3. Write 3 equivalent fractions for each fraction.

   a) $\frac{2}{3}$ = ____ = ____ = ____   b) $\frac{24}{36}$ = ____ = ____ = ____

   c) $\frac{36}{72}$ = ____ = ____ = ____   d) $\frac{4}{7}$ = ____ = ____ = ____

4. Write each fraction in simpler form.

   a) $\frac{9}{12}$ = ____   b) $\frac{6}{15}$ = ____   c) $\frac{45}{60}$ = ____   d) $\frac{36}{48}$ = ____

   e) $\frac{60}{100}$ = ____   f) $\frac{45}{54}$ = ____   g) $\frac{30}{70}$ = ____   h) $\frac{42}{48}$ = ____

5. Write each fraction in simplest form.

   a) $\frac{6}{8}$ = ____   b) $\frac{49}{56}$ = ____   c) $\frac{24}{36}$ = ____   d) $\frac{45}{75}$ = ____

   e) $\frac{27}{54}$ = ____   f) $\frac{54}{60}$ = ____   g) $\frac{8}{9}$ = ____   h) $\frac{12}{18}$ = ____

6. Circle the fractions that are in simplest form.

   $\frac{29}{58}$ $\frac{27}{64}$ $\frac{14}{53}$ $\frac{30}{60}$ $\frac{13}{52}$ $\frac{28}{36}$ $\frac{21}{43}$ $\frac{90}{110}$

Stretch Your Thinking . . . .

Use the digits 1, 2, 3, 4, 6, and 8 to make a fraction equivalent to $\frac{1}{2}$.
You must use all of the digits and you can use each digit only once.
Do this in as many ways as you can.

_____

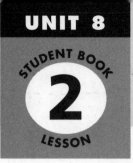

Relating Mixed Numbers and Improper Fractions

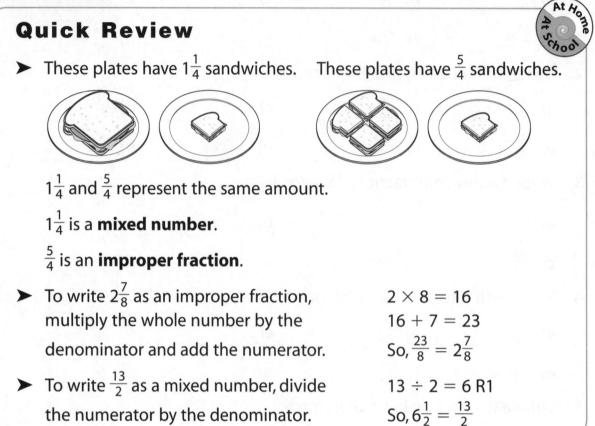

Quick Review

➤ These plates have $1\frac{1}{4}$ sandwiches.　These plates have $\frac{5}{4}$ sandwiches.

$1\frac{1}{4}$ and $\frac{5}{4}$ represent the same amount.

$1\frac{1}{4}$ is a **mixed number**.

$\frac{5}{4}$ is an **improper fraction**.

➤ To write $2\frac{7}{8}$ as an improper fraction, multiply the whole number by the denominator and add the numerator.

$2 \times 8 = 16$
$16 + 7 = 23$
So, $\frac{23}{8} = 2\frac{7}{8}$

➤ To write $\frac{13}{2}$ as a mixed number, divide the numerator by the denominator.

$13 \div 2 = 6 \text{ R1}$
So, $6\frac{1}{2} = \frac{13}{2}$

Try These

1. Write each mixed number as an improper fraction.

   a) $3\frac{7}{9} = $ _____　　b) $4\frac{3}{4} = $ _____　　c) $7\frac{6}{11} = $ _____　　d) $1\frac{19}{20} = $ _____

2. Write each improper fraction as a mixed number.

   a) $\frac{8}{5} = $ _____　　b) $\frac{39}{7} = $ _____　　c) $\frac{48}{9} = $ _____　　d) $\frac{16}{3} = $ _____

Play this game with a partner.
You will need 1 number cube, 2 game markers, and 24 small counters.

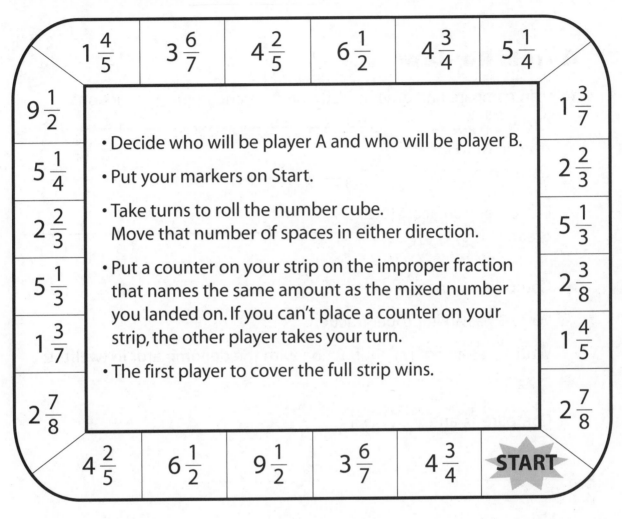

On the game board:

$1\frac{4}{5}$ $3\frac{6}{7}$ $4\frac{2}{5}$ $6\frac{1}{2}$ $4\frac{3}{4}$ $5\frac{1}{4}$

$9\frac{1}{2}$ $1\frac{3}{7}$

$5\frac{1}{4}$ $2\frac{2}{3}$

$2\frac{2}{3}$ $5\frac{1}{3}$

$5\frac{1}{3}$ $2\frac{3}{8}$

$1\frac{3}{7}$ $1\frac{4}{5}$

$2\frac{7}{8}$ $2\frac{7}{8}$

$4\frac{2}{5}$ $6\frac{1}{2}$ $9\frac{1}{2}$ $3\frac{6}{7}$ $4\frac{3}{4}$ **START**

- Decide who will be player A and who will be player B.
- Put your markers on Start.
- Take turns to roll the number cube.
  Move that number of spaces in either direction.
- Put a counter on your strip on the improper fraction that names the same amount as the mixed number you landed on. If you can't place a counter on your strip, the other player takes your turn.
- The first player to cover the full strip wins.

Player A	$\frac{22}{5}$	$\frac{8}{3}$	$\frac{13}{2}$	$\frac{16}{3}$	$\frac{9}{5}$	$\frac{19}{4}$	$\frac{19}{2}$	$\frac{27}{7}$	$\frac{19}{8}$	$\frac{21}{4}$	$\frac{23}{8}$	$\frac{10}{7}$
Player B	$\frac{22}{5}$	$\frac{8}{3}$	$\frac{13}{2}$	$\frac{16}{3}$	$\frac{9}{5}$	$\frac{19}{4}$	$\frac{19}{2}$	$\frac{27}{7}$	$\frac{19}{8}$	$\frac{21}{4}$	$\frac{23}{8}$	$\frac{10}{7}$

Stretch Your Thinking

Sadie says she has $\frac{7}{4}$ dollars. How much money does she have? Explain.

_____

_____

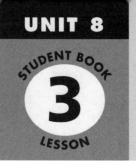

Comparing and Ordering Mixed Numbers and Fractions

Quick Review

At Home
At School

You can compare and order mixed numbers and improper fractions.

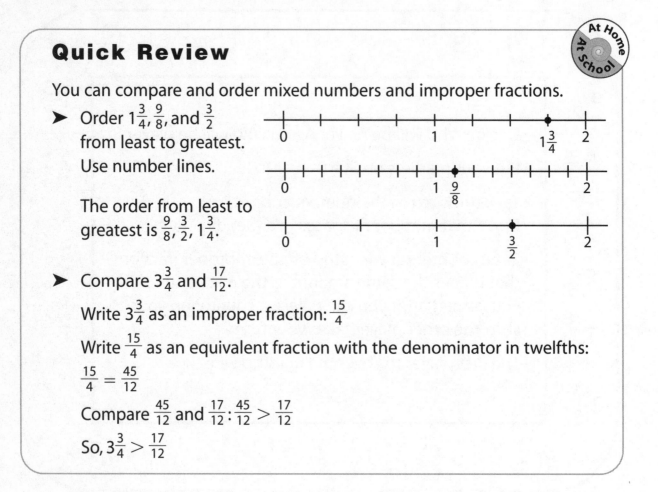

➤ Order $1\frac{3}{4}, \frac{9}{8},$ and $\frac{3}{2}$ from least to greatest. Use number lines.

The order from least to greatest is $\frac{9}{8}, \frac{3}{2}, 1\frac{3}{4}$.

➤ Compare $3\frac{3}{4}$ and $\frac{17}{12}$.

Write $3\frac{3}{4}$ as an improper fraction: $\frac{15}{4}$

Write $\frac{15}{4}$ as an equivalent fraction with the denominator in twelfths:

$\frac{15}{4} = \frac{45}{12}$

Compare $\frac{45}{12}$ and $\frac{17}{12}$: $\frac{45}{12} > \frac{17}{12}$

So, $3\frac{3}{4} > \frac{17}{12}$

Try These

1. Use these number lines to order $\frac{5}{3}, 1\frac{1}{6},$ and $\frac{3}{2}$ from least to greatest.

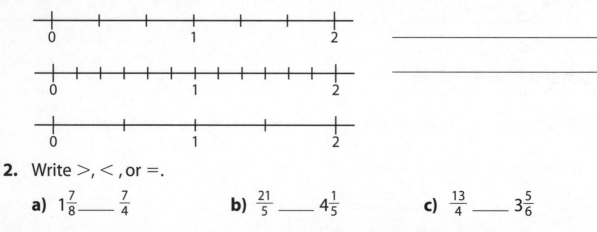

_____

_____

2. Write $>, <,$ or $=$.

a) $1\frac{7}{8}$ _____ $\frac{7}{4}$

b) $\frac{21}{5}$ _____ $4\frac{1}{5}$

c) $\frac{13}{4}$ _____ $3\frac{5}{6}$

1. Write $>$, $<$, or $=$.

    a) $\frac{11}{7}$ _____ $\frac{10}{9}$

    b) $\frac{21}{8}$ _____ $\frac{31}{12}$

    c) $\frac{17}{7}$ _____ $2\frac{3}{4}$

    d) $1\frac{1}{2}$ _____ $\frac{24}{16}$

    e) $\frac{24}{5}$ _____ $\frac{48}{10}$

    f) $3\frac{4}{5}$ _____ $\frac{78}{25}$

2. Use a mixed number to complete each question.

    a) $\frac{9}{4} =$ _____

    b) $\frac{19}{11} >$ _____

    c) $\frac{25}{12} <$ _____

    d) $\frac{41}{3} <$ _____

    e) $\frac{30}{10} <$ _____

    f) $\frac{14}{3} >$ _____

3. Order the numbers in each set from greatest to least.

    a) $\frac{8}{3}, 1\frac{11}{12}, \frac{7}{4}$ _____

    b) $\frac{10}{6}, \frac{8}{8}, 1\frac{1}{3}$ _____

    c) $\frac{9}{5}, \frac{11}{10}, 1\frac{7}{20}$ _____

    d) $2\frac{8}{12}, \frac{13}{6}, \frac{9}{8}$ _____

4. Use these number lines to order $\frac{5}{2}$, $2\frac{1}{4}$, and $\frac{6}{3}$ from greatest to least.

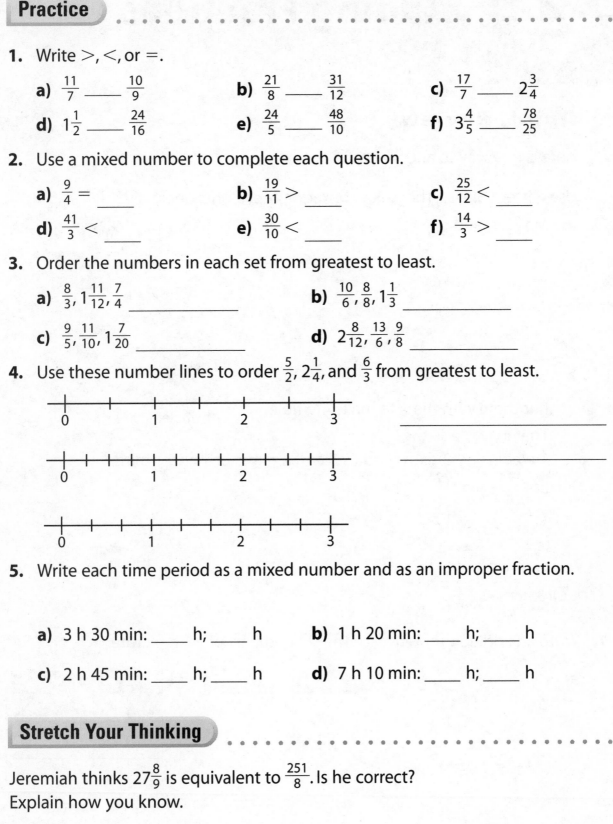

5. Write each time period as a mixed number and as an improper fraction.

    a) 3 h 30 min: _____ h; _____ h

    b) 1 h 20 min: _____ h; _____ h

    c) 2 h 45 min: _____ h; _____ h

    d) 7 h 10 min: _____ h; _____ h

Stretch Your Thinking

Jeremiah thinks $27\frac{8}{9}$ is equivalent to $\frac{251}{8}$. Is he correct?
Explain how you know.

_____

_____

Adding Fractions

Name

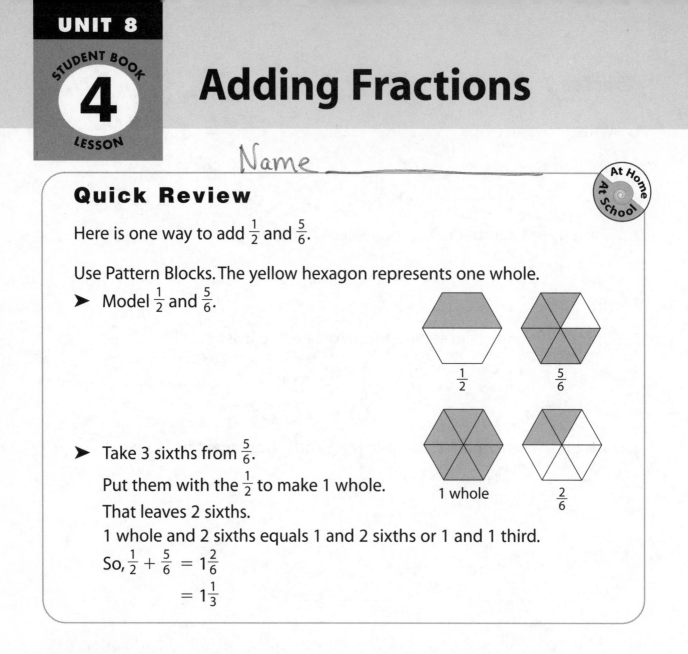

Quick Review

Here is one way to add $\frac{1}{2}$ and $\frac{5}{6}$.

Use Pattern Blocks. The yellow hexagon represents one whole.

➤ Model $\frac{1}{2}$ and $\frac{5}{6}$.

$\frac{1}{2}$ $\frac{5}{6}$

➤ Take 3 sixths from $\frac{5}{6}$.

Put them with the $\frac{1}{2}$ to make 1 whole.

That leaves 2 sixths.

1 whole and 2 sixths equals 1 and 2 sixths or 1 and 1 third.

So, $\frac{1}{2} + \frac{5}{6} = 1\frac{2}{6}$

$= 1\frac{1}{3}$

1 whole $\frac{2}{6}$

Try These

1. Write an addition sentence for the shaded part of each picture.

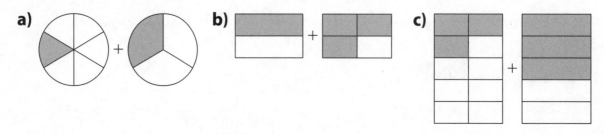

a)   b)   c)

1. Colour the Pattern Blocks to find each sum.

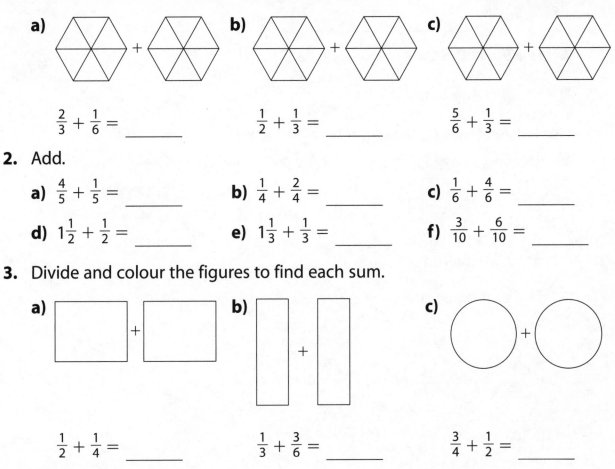

   a) $\frac{2}{3} + \frac{1}{6} =$ _____

   b) $\frac{1}{2} + \frac{1}{3} =$ _____

   c) $\frac{5}{6} + \frac{1}{3} =$ _____

2. Add.

   a) $\frac{4}{5} + \frac{1}{5} =$ _____

   b) $\frac{1}{4} + \frac{2}{4} =$ _____

   c) $\frac{1}{6} + \frac{4}{6} =$ _____

   d) $1\frac{1}{2} + \frac{1}{2} =$ _____

   e) $1\frac{1}{3} + \frac{1}{3} =$ _____

   f) $\frac{3}{10} + \frac{6}{10} =$ _____

3. Divide and colour the figures to find each sum.

   a) $\frac{1}{2} + \frac{1}{4} =$ _____

   b) $\frac{1}{3} + \frac{3}{6} =$ _____

   c) $\frac{3}{4} + \frac{1}{2} =$ _____

4. Draw a diagram to find each sum.

   $\frac{1}{4} + \frac{5}{8} =$ _____

   $\frac{1}{2} + \frac{1}{4} =$ _____

   $\frac{1}{3} + \frac{5}{6} =$ _____

Stretch Your Thinking

Neema has 3 dimes and 2 quarters. What fraction of a dollar does she have?

_____

Subtracting Fractions

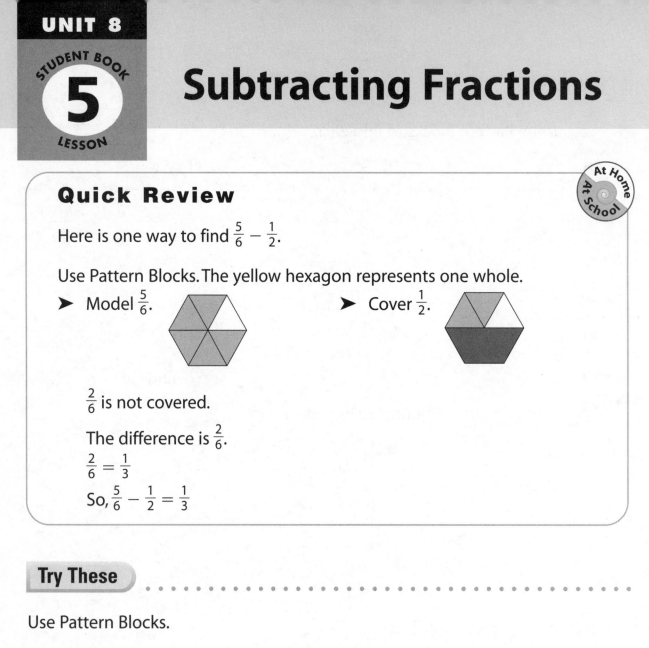

Quick Review

At Home
At School

Here is one way to find $\frac{5}{6} - \frac{1}{2}$.

Use Pattern Blocks. The yellow hexagon represents one whole.

➤ Model $\frac{5}{6}$.

➤ Cover $\frac{1}{2}$.

$\frac{2}{6}$ is not covered.

The difference is $\frac{2}{6}$.

$\frac{2}{6} = \frac{1}{3}$

So, $\frac{5}{6} - \frac{1}{2} = \frac{1}{3}$

Try These

Use Pattern Blocks.

1. Subtract.

   a) $\frac{1}{2} - \frac{1}{3} = $ _____

   b) $\frac{5}{6} - \frac{4}{6} = $ _____

   c) $\frac{2}{3} - \frac{1}{2} = $ _____

   d) $\frac{2}{3} - \frac{2}{6} = $ _____

   e) $\frac{1}{2} - \frac{1}{6} = $ _____

   f) $\frac{1}{2} - \frac{3}{6} = $ _____

2. Is each difference greater than $\frac{1}{2}$ or less than $\frac{1}{2}$? Explain how you know.

   a) $\frac{5}{6} - \frac{1}{6}$ _____

   b) $1 - \frac{1}{3}$ _____

   c) $\frac{5}{6} - \frac{1}{2}$ _____

   d) $\frac{1}{3} - \frac{1}{6}$ _____

1. Use the diagrams to find each difference.

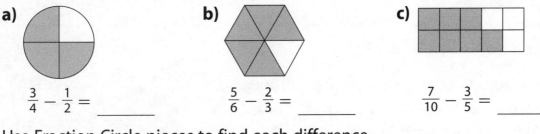

   a)

   $\frac{3}{4} - \frac{1}{2} =$ _____

   b)

   $\frac{5}{6} - \frac{2}{3} =$ _____

   c)

   $\frac{7}{10} - \frac{3}{5} =$ _____

2. Use Fraction Circle pieces to find each difference.

   a) $\frac{9}{10} - \frac{2}{5} =$ _____   **b)** $\frac{5}{8} - \frac{1}{4} =$ _____   **c)** $1 - \frac{2}{3} =$ _____

   d) $2 - \frac{3}{4} =$ _____   **e)** $\frac{4}{5} - \frac{1}{2} =$ _____   **f)** $\frac{1}{2} - \frac{1}{4} =$ _____

3. Sergio has $\frac{7}{8}$ cup of trail mix. He gives Lien $\frac{3}{4}$ cup.
   How much does he have left? Use pictures, numbers, and words.

   _____

   _____

4. Kate drank $\frac{7}{10}$ glass of buttermilk. Vicky drank $\frac{4}{5}$ glass.

   a) Who drank more buttermilk? _____

   Explain. _____

   b) How much more did she drink? Explain how you know.

   _____

Stretch Your Thinking

Armin has 3 flower gardens. He bought 5 bags of cedar mulch to cover the
gardens. He used $1\frac{1}{2}$ bags of mulch on each garden. How much mulch does
Armin have left?

_____

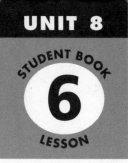
Exploring Percents

Quick Review

At Home
At School

This hundredths grid has 100 small squares.
Each square represents $\frac{1}{100}$ of the grid.
Twenty-seven squares are shaded.

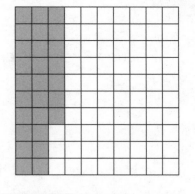

You can describe the shaded part of the grid.

➤ 27 out of 100 squares are shaded.

➤ $\frac{27}{100}$ of the grid is shaded.

➤ 0.27 of the grid is shaded.

➤ 27% of the grid is shaded.

Percent means "per hundred" or "out of 100."

This is a **percent** symbol. You read 27% as 27 percent.

Try These

1. Write a fraction with hundredths, a decimal, and a percent to describe the shaded part of each grid.

   a)   b)   c)   d)

   _____   _____   _____   _____

2. Write a fraction with hundredths, a decimal, and a percent to describe the unshaded part of each grid in question 1.

   a) _____ b) _____ c) _____ d) _____

1. Colour each hundredths grid to show the percent.

   a) 42%

   b) 75%

   c) 6%

2. **a)** Use the hundredths grid. Colour 35% blue, 7% red, 40% green, and the rest orange.

   b) Write a fraction and a decimal to describe each colour.

   blue _____   red _____

   green _____   orange _____

   c) What percent is orange? _____

3. Write as a percent and as a decimal.

   a) $\frac{43}{100}$ _____ _____

   b) $\frac{16}{100}$ _____ _____

   c) $\frac{100}{100}$ _____ _____

   d) $\frac{3}{100}$ _____ _____

   e) $\frac{82}{100}$ _____ _____

   f) $\frac{11}{100}$ _____ _____

4. Write as a fraction and as a decimal.

   a) 19% _____ _____

   b) 1% _____ _____

   c) 93% _____ _____

   d) 7% _____ _____

   e) 100% _____ _____

   f) 47% _____ _____

Stretch Your Thinking

Draw a rectangle and an oval around groups of Xs so that all of the following statements are true.
- 64% of the Xs are not inside either figure.
- 8% of the Xs are inside both figures.
- 20% of the Xs are inside the rectangle only.
- 8% of the Xs are inside the oval only.

Relating Fractions, Decimals, and Percents

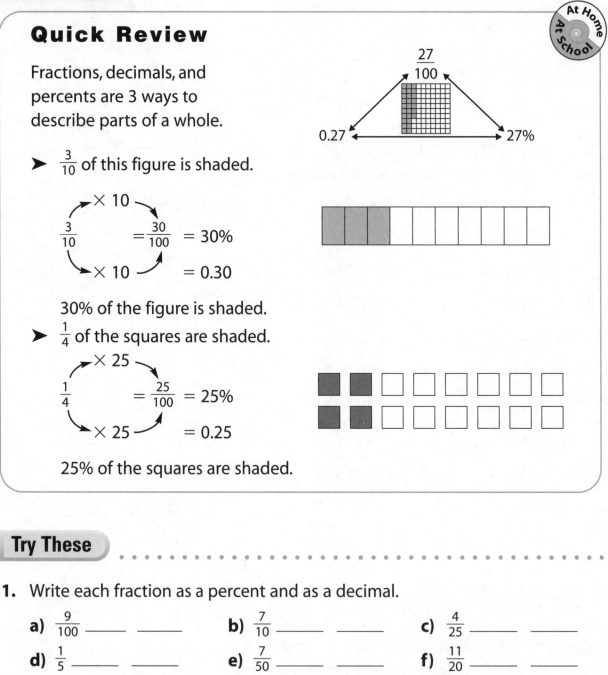

Quick Review

Fractions, decimals, and percents are 3 ways to describe parts of a whole.

➤ $\frac{3}{10}$ of this figure is shaded.

$$\frac{3}{10} = \frac{30}{100} = 30\%$$
$$\times 10$$
$$\times 10$$
$$= 0.30$$

30% of the figure is shaded.

➤ $\frac{1}{4}$ of the squares are shaded.

$$\frac{1}{4} = \frac{25}{100} = 25\%$$
$$\times 25$$
$$\times 25$$
$$= 0.25$$

25% of the squares are shaded.

$$\frac{27}{100}$$
$$0.27 \qquad 27\%$$

Try These

1. Write each fraction as a percent and as a decimal.

   a) $\frac{9}{100}$ _____ _____

   b) $\frac{7}{10}$ _____ _____

   c) $\frac{4}{25}$ _____ _____

   d) $\frac{1}{5}$ _____ _____

   e) $\frac{7}{50}$ _____ _____

   f) $\frac{11}{20}$ _____ _____

2. What percent is shaded?

   a)

   b)

   c)

   _____   _____   _____

1. **a)** Use the hundredths grid to make a design. Follow these rules:

   ➤ You can use only red, black, green, and blue.

   ➤ You must colour at least $\frac{7}{10}$ of the squares.

   ➤ You must use:
   - red for at least 6% of the squares.
   - black for at least 5% of the squares.
   - green and blue together for at least 0.4 of the squares.

   b) Complete the chart to describe the colours in your design.

Colour	Red	Black	Green	Blue	No Colour
Number of Squares					
Fraction					
Decimal					
Percent of Grid					

   c) What is the greatest percent of blank squares you could have in your design? Explain.

   _____

   _____

   d) What is the sum of your decimals? _____ Percents? _____

   What do you think the sum of your fractions would be? _____

Stretch Your Thinking

What percent of Canada's ten provinces begin with a vowel? With a consonant? Explain.

_____

_____

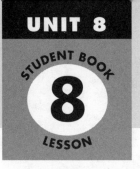
Estimating and Finding a Percent

Name

At Home
At School

Quick Review

➤ To estimate 20% of 89:
Round 89 to 90.

Find 20% of 90.

$20\% = \frac{20}{100}$, or $\frac{1}{5}$

$\frac{1}{5}$ of 90 $= \frac{90}{5} = 18$

So, 20% of 89 is about 18.

➤ To estimate what
percent 19 is of 40:

20 is $\frac{1}{2}$ of 40.

So, 19 is almost $\frac{1}{2}$ of 40.

$\frac{1}{2} = \frac{50}{100} = 50\%$

So, 19 is almost 50% of 40.

➤ Here are 2 ways to find 30% of $80:

$30\% = \frac{30}{100}$, or $\frac{3}{10}$

$$\frac{3}{10} \xrightarrow{\times 8} = \frac{24}{80} \xleftarrow{\times 8}$$

So, 30% of $80 is $24.

$30\% = \frac{30}{100}$, or $\frac{3}{10}$

$\frac{1}{10}$ of 80 $= \frac{80}{10} = 8$

$\frac{3}{10}$ of 80 $= 3 \times 8$

$= 24$

So, 30% of $80 is $24.

Try These

1. Estimate.

   a) 50% of 79 _____ **b)** 25% of 58 _____ **c)** 10% of 99 _____

   d) 9% of 60 _____ **e)** 11% of 60 _____ **f)** 24% of 36 _____

2. Find each amount.

   a) 10% of 48 = _____ **b)** 25% of 60 = _____ **c)** 50% of 66 = _____

   d) 75% of 160 = _____ **e)** 80% of 200 = _____ **f)** 40% of 150 = _____

Name _____

1. Estimate.

   a) 10% of 89 _____   **b)** 19% of 40 _____   **c)** 25% of $198 _____

   d) 9% of 80 _____   **e)** 70% of 31 _____   **f)** 49% of $201 _____

2. Find each amount. Then use the letters next to the amounts to solve this riddle.

What kind of table has no legs?

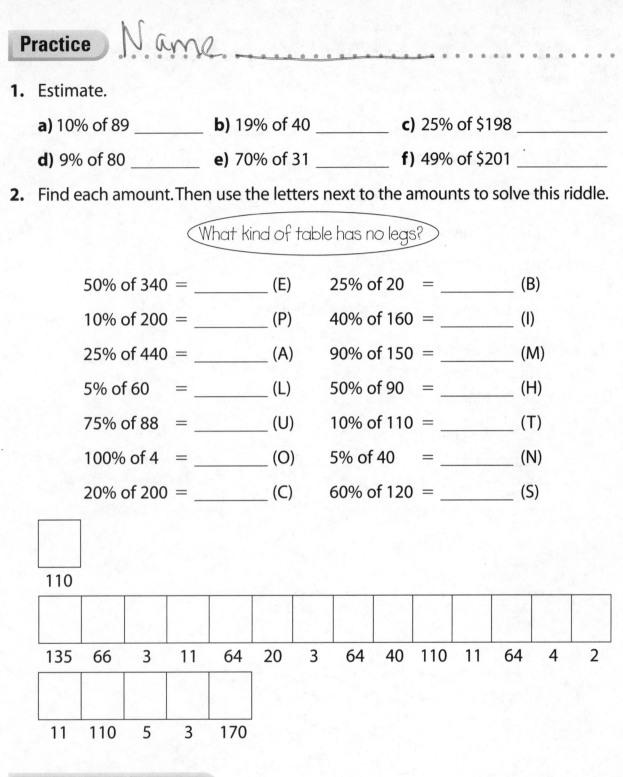

50% of 340 = _____ (E)   25% of 20 = _____ (B)

10% of 200 = _____ (P)   40% of 160 = _____ (I)

25% of 440 = _____ (A)   90% of 150 = _____ (M)

5% of 60 = _____ (L)   50% of 90 = _____ (H)

75% of 88 = _____ (U)   10% of 110 = _____ (T)

100% of 4 = _____ (O)   5% of 40 = _____ (N)

20% of 200 = _____ (C)   60% of 120 = _____ (S)

110

135   66   3   11   64   20   3   64   40   110   11   64   4   2

11   110   5   3   170

Stretch Your Thinking

Thirty percent of the answers to a survey question were "Yes."
If 87 people said "Yes," how many people were surveyed? Explain.

_____

_____

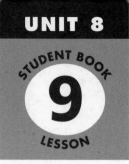

Exploring Ratios

Quick Review

At Home At School

A **ratio** is a comparison of 2 quantities with the same unit.

Here are 3 squares and 5 circles.

☐ ☐ ☐ ○ ○ ○ ○ ○

Here are some ways to compare the figures.

➤ Part-to-Part Ratios
  • squares to circles is 3 to 5 or 3 : 5.
  • circles to squares is 5 to 3 or 5 : 3.

> The numbers 3 and 5 are the **terms of the ratio**.

➤ Part-to-Whole Ratios
  • squares to figures is 3 to 8 or 3 : 8 or $\frac{3}{8}$.
  • circles to figures is 5 to 8 or 5 : 8 or $\frac{5}{8}$.

> You can write a part-to-whole ratio as a fraction.

Try These

1. Write each ratio in as many ways as you can.

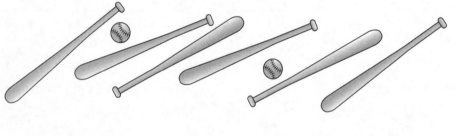

   a) balls to bats _____

   b) bats to balls _____

   c) balls to all toys _____

   d) bats to all toys _____

1. Use the numbers in the box to write each ratio.

   a) odd numbers to even numbers _____

   b) numbers less than 20 to all numbers _____

   c) multiples of 5 to multiples of 7 _____

   d) prime numbers to composite numbers _____

25	16	13	38
17	30	49	3
24	45	7	14

2. Write a word that has each ratio of vowels to consonants.

   a) 2:5 _____   **b)** 1:4 _____   **c)** 4:6 _____

3. What is being compared in each ratio?

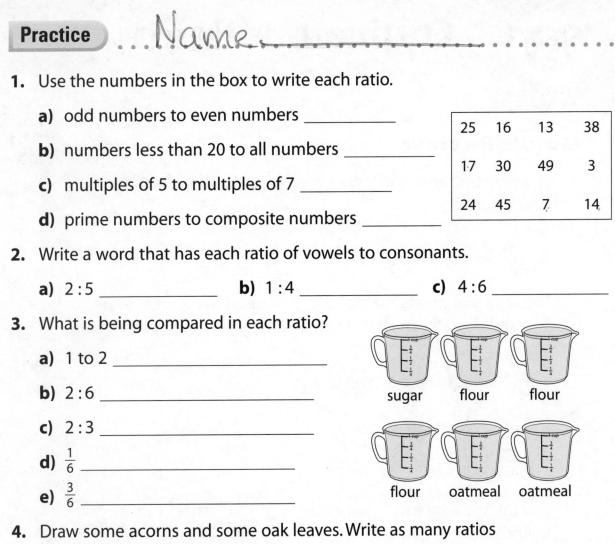

sugar   flour   flour

flour   oatmeal   oatmeal

   a) 1 to 2 _____

   b) 2:6 _____

   c) 2:3 _____

   d) $\frac{1}{6}$ _____

   e) $\frac{3}{6}$ _____

4. Draw some acorns and some oak leaves. Write as many ratios as you can for your drawing.

   _____   _____   _____

   _____   _____   _____

Stretch Your Thinking ....

Ask 5 people to name the sport they enjoy watching the most.
Write as many ratios as you can to compare the responses.
Tell what each ratio compares.

_____

_____

_____

_____

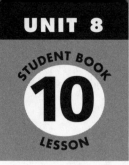

Equivalent Ratios

Quick Review

➤ The ratio 3 : 2 means that for every 3 apples there are 2 pears.

The ratio 6 : 4 means that for every 6 apples there are 4 pears.
3 : 2 and 6 : 4 are equal. 3 : 2 and 6 : 4 are **equivalent ratios**.

➤ You can use a table and patterns
to find equivalent ratios.
The numbers in the apples
column are multiples of 3.
The numbers in the pears
column are multiples of 2.
The ratios of apples to pears are:
3 : 2, 6 : 4, 9 : 6, 12 : 8, 15 : 10, …

Apples	Pears	Ratio
3	2	3 : 2
6	4	6 : 4
9	6	9 : 6
12	8	12 : 8
15	10	15 : 10

Try These

1. Write 2 equivalent ratios for each ratio.

   a) 5 : 3 _____ _____   **b)** 7 : 4 _____ _____   **c)** 3 : 9 _____ _____

   d) 4 : 11 _____ _____   **e)** 2 : 6 _____ _____   **f)** 8 : 5 _____ _____

Practice

1. Play this game with a partner.
   You will need 2 sheets of paper and a clock or watch with a second hand.

   ➤ Player A chooses a ratio and writes as many equivalent ratios as she can, as Player B times 30 s.
   ➤ Both players check Player A's ratios.
     Player A gets 1 point for each correct ratio.
   ➤ Players switch roles and play again, using a different ratio.
   ➤ The player with the most points after 5 rounds wins.

Ratios	
3 : 7	7 : 4
2 : 5	2 : 9
6 : 3	12 : 11
4 : 3	10 : 15
8 : 6	3 : 8

2. Write an equivalent ratio with 30 as one of the terms.

   a) 15 : 7 _____ **b)** 8 : 5 _____ **c)** 2 : 6 _____ **d)** 3 : 14 _____

   e) 11 : 5 _____ **f)** 3 : 2 _____ **g)** 4 : 10 _____ **h)** 18 : 15 _____

3. List all the ratios that are equivalent to 4 : 7 and have a first term that is less

   than 25. _____

4. Jillian is planting 4 roses for every 3 daisies in her garden.
   Complete the table to show how many daisies Jillian needs for 8, 12, and 16 roses.
   Write each ratio.

Roses	Daisies	Ratio
4	3	

Stretch Your Thinking

Mr. Tanaka has 56 students in his choir. The ratio of boys to girls is 3 : 4.
How many boys and how many girls are in Mr. Tanaka's choir? Explain.

_____

_____

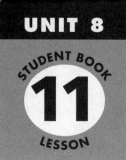

UNIT 8

STUDENT BOOK 11 LESSON

Exploring Rates

Quick Review

At Home At School

➤ If your heart beats 75 times in 1 min, your heart **rate** is *75 beats per minute*. We write this as *75 beats/min*.
Here are some other rates:

A **rate** is a ratio that compares 2 items measured in different units.

• Cody types 50 words/min.
• The eggs cost $1.59/dozen.
• Sound travels about 330 m/s.
• Helen walks 4 km/h.

➤ A train travels at a speed of 75 km/h.
How far does it travel in 5 h?
Here are 2 ways to solve this rate problem.

Draw a graph.

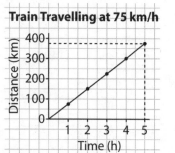

Make a table.

Distance (km)	Time (h)
75	1
150	2
225	3
300	4
375	5

The train travels 375 km in 5 h.

Try These

1. Write each amount as a rate.

   a) A cereal contains 4 scoops of raisins in each kg. _____

   b) Bert did 40 jumping jacks in 1 min. _____

   c) The radio station plays 15 songs per hour. _____

130

1. Kenisha drove at an average speed of 90 km/h.
   At this rate, how far did she travel in 4 h? _____

2. Missie's Dance School charges $8 per lesson.
   How much would Dan pay for 5 lessons? _____

3. A caterpillar crawled 4 m in 15 min. At that rate, how long will it take

   the caterpillar to travel 6 m? _____

4. Express each speed in kilometres per hour.

   a) A bat travels 75 km in 3 h. _____

   b) An elephant walks 2.5 km in half an hour. _____

   c) A car travels 280 km in 4 h. _____

   d) A truck travels 1 km in 1 min. _____

5. Abel picks 2 baskets of berries in 15 min.
   Lucy picks 3 baskets in 18 min.
   Which person picks more berries every minute?

   Explain. _____

   _____

6. Sebastian runs 15 km every 4 days.
   Complete the table to find how long it takes Sebastian to run over 100 km.

Distance (km)	15	30					
Time (days)	4	8					

Stretch Your Thinking . . . .

String licorice costs $1.77 for 3 m. How much licorice could Patu buy with $9?

Perimeter

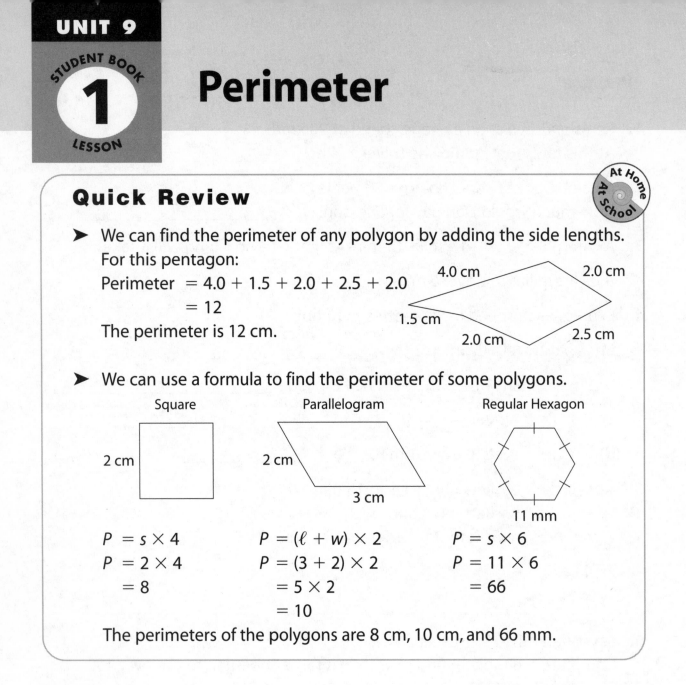

At Home
At School

Quick Review

➤ We can find the perimeter of any polygon by adding the side lengths.
For this pentagon:

Perimeter = 4.0 + 1.5 + 2.0 + 2.5 + 2.0

= 12

The perimeter is 12 cm.

4.0 cm   2.0 cm

1.5 cm

2.0 cm   2.5 cm

➤ We can use a formula to find the perimeter of some polygons.

Square	Parallelogram	Regular Hexagon

2 cm

2 cm

3 cm

11 mm

$P = s \times 4$ $P = (\ell + w) \times 2$ $P = s \times 6$

$P = 2 \times 4$ $P = (3 + 2) \times 2$ $P = 11 \times 6$

= 8   = 5 × 2   = 66

= 10

The perimeters of the polygons are 8 cm, 10 cm, and 66 mm.

Try These

1. Find the perimeter of each polygon.

a)

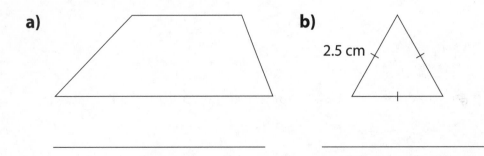

b)

2.5 cm

_____

_____

_____

_____

Practice

1. Find the perimeter of each polygon.

   a) **b)** **c)**

   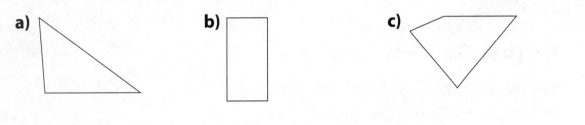

   _____   _____   _____

   _____   _____   _____

2. Kerry skates laps around the playground.
   The playground is 150 m long and 50 m wide.
   How many laps will it take Kerry to skate 1 km? _____

   _____

3. The perimeter of an equilateral triangle is 5.1 dm. How long are its sides?
   Give your answer in as many different units as you can.

   _____

   _____

4. The perimeter of an atlas is 1.4 m.
   How long might each side be? _____

   _____

5. Suppose the side lengths of a rectangle are halved.
   What would happen to the perimeter?

   _____

Stretch Your Thinking

One side of Kirby's rectangular
garden measures 5 m.
The perimeter of the garden is 27 m.
Draw a sketch of Kirby's garden.
Label the side lengths.

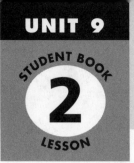

Exploring Rectangles

Quick Review

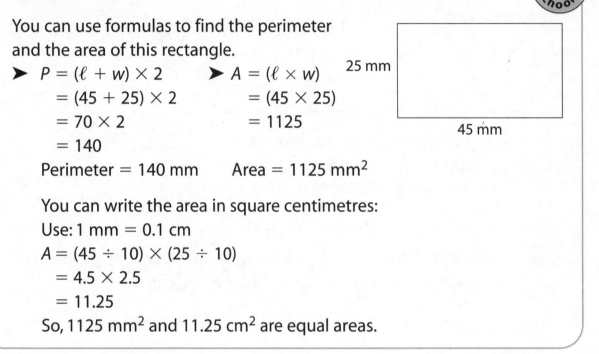

You can use formulas to find the perimeter and the area of this rectangle.

➤ $P = (\ell + w) \times 2$ ➤ $A = (\ell \times w)$
    $= (45 + 25) \times 2$ $= (45 \times 25)$
    $= 70 \times 2$ $= 1125$
    $= 140$
   Perimeter = 140 mm   Area = 1125 mm^2

You can write the area in square centimetres:
Use: 1 mm = 0.1 cm
$A = (45 \div 10) \times (25 \div 10)$
    $= 4.5 \times 2.5$
    $= 11.25$
So, 1125 mm^2 and 11.25 cm^2 are equal areas.

Try These

1. Find the perimeter of each rectangle in centimetres and in millimetres.
   Then find each area in square centimetres and in square millimetres.

   Perimeter of A: _____

   Area of A: _____

   Perimeter of B: _____

   Area of B: _____

   Perimeter of C: _____

   Area of C: _____

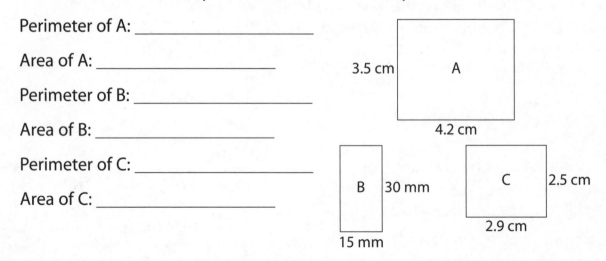

1. The perimeter of a placemat is 1489 mm. How many centimetres is that?

   _____

2. Find the perimeter and area of each rectangle.
   Record each measure in two different units.

   a)

   3.3 km

   2.0 km

   b)

   3.0 dm

   4.1 dm

   _____   _____

   _____   _____

3. The area of a rectangular ballroom is 800 m² and the perimeter is 120 m.
   What are the dimensions of the ballroom? _____

   _____

4. The area of a rug is 8000 cm². How many square metres is that?

   _____

The length of a rectangle is increased by 1 unit. Its width is decreased by 1 unit.
What happens to the area and the perimeter?
Use an example in your explanation.

_____

_____

_____

_____

_____

_____

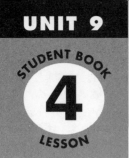
Area of a Parallelogram

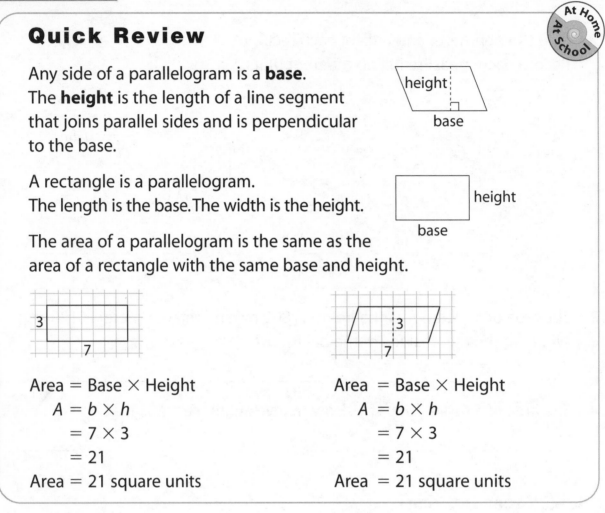

Quick Review

Any side of a parallelogram is a **base**.
The **height** is the length of a line segment
that joins parallel sides and is perpendicular
to the base.

height
base

A rectangle is a parallelogram.
The length is the base. The width is the height.

height
base

The area of a parallelogram is the same as the
area of a rectangle with the same base and height.

3
7

3
7

Area = Base × Height
$A = b \times h$
$= 7 \times 3$
$= 21$
Area = 21 square units

Area = Base × Height
$A = b \times h$
$= 7 \times 3$
$= 21$
Area = 21 square units

Try These

1. For each parallelogram, draw a rectangle with the same base and height.
   Then find the area of each parallelogram.

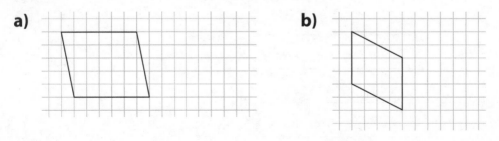

   a)

   b)

1. Find the area of each parallelogram.

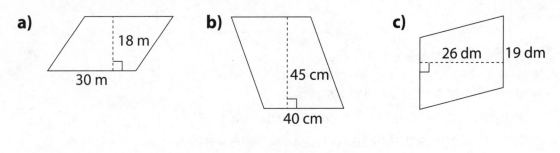

a)

18 m

30 m

b)

45 cm

40 cm

c)

26 dm   19 dm

_____   _____   _____

2. Find the length of the base or the height of each parallelogram.

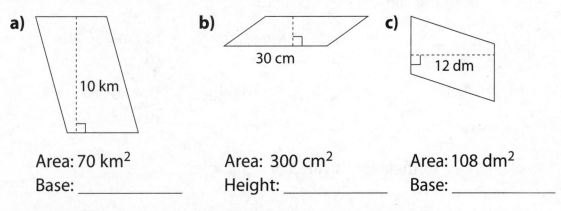

a)

10 km

b)

30 cm

c)

12 dm

Area: 70 km²
Base: _____

Area: 300 cm²
Height: _____

Area: 108 dm²
Base: _____

3. Draw 3 different parallelograms with area 18 square units.

Draw a parallelogram with
base 3 cm and height 2 cm.
Then draw a parallelogram
with twice the area.

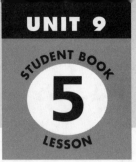
Exploring Triangles and Rectangles

Quick Review

At Home
At School

Any side of a triangle can be its base.
The height of a triangle is the perpendicular line segment that joins the base to the opposite vertex.

height

base

The area of a triangle is one-half the area of the rectangle with the same base and height.

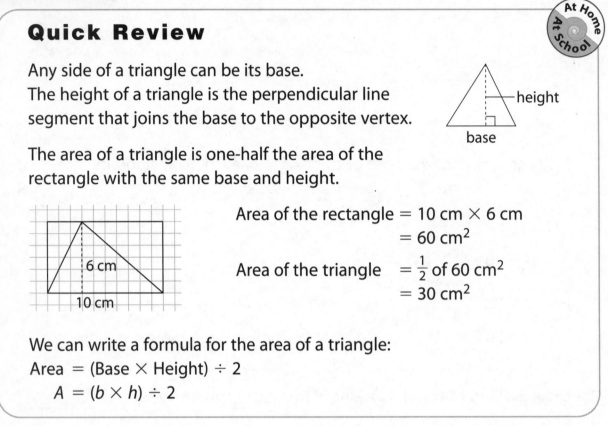

Area of the rectangle = 10 cm × 6 cm
= 60 cm^2

Area of the triangle = $\frac{1}{2}$ of 60 cm^2
= 30 cm^2

We can write a formula for the area of a triangle:
Area = (Base × Height) ÷ 2
$A = (b \times h) \div 2$

Try These ·

1. Find the area of each triangle in square units.

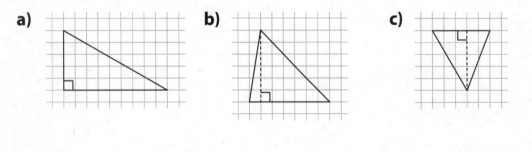

a)

b)

c)

_____

_____

_____

_____

_____

_____

1. Estimate, then find the area of each triangle.

   a)

   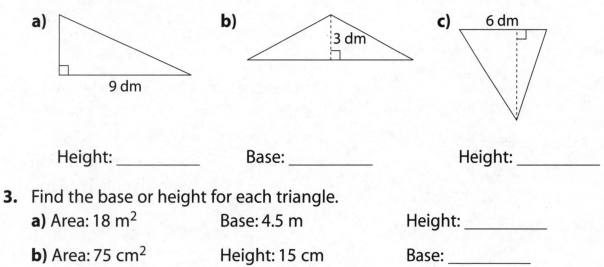

   b)

   Estimate: _____   Estimate: _____

   Area: _____   Area: _____

2. Each triangle has area 18 dm². Find each base or height.

   a)   **b)**   **c)**

   9 dm   3 dm   6 dm

   Height: _____   Base: _____   Height: _____

3. Find the base or height for each triangle.
   a) Area: 18 m²   Base: 4.5 m   Height: _____

   b) Area: 75 cm²   Height: 15 cm   Base: _____

Stretch Your Thinking . . . .

Draw 4 different triangles with area 8 square units.

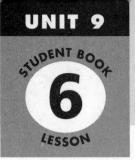

UNIT 9

STUDENT BOOK

6

LESSON

Exploring Triangles and Parallelograms

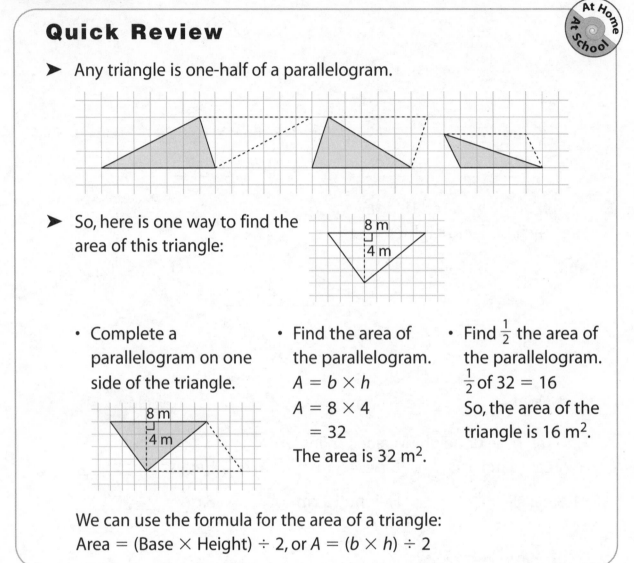

Quick Review

➤ Any triangle is one-half of a parallelogram.

➤ So, here is one way to find the area of this triangle:

8 m
4 m

• Complete a parallelogram on one side of the triangle.

8 m
4 m

• Find the area of the parallelogram.

$A = b \times h$

$A = 8 \times 4$

$ = 32$

The area is 32 m².

• Find $\frac{1}{2}$ the area of the parallelogram.

$\frac{1}{2}$ of 32 = 16

So, the area of the triangle is 16 m².

We can use the formula for the area of a triangle:

Area = (Base × Height) ÷ 2, or $A = (b \times h) \div 2$

Try These

1. Complete a parallelogram on one side of each triangle.

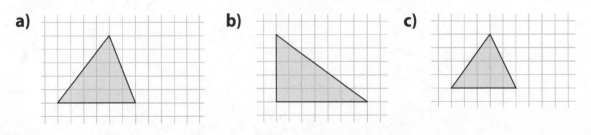

a)

b)

c)

Practice

1. Find the area of each triangle.

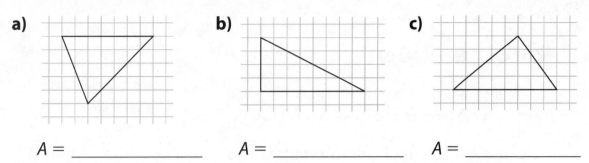

a)

b)

c)

$A =$ _____ $A =$ _____ $A =$ _____

2. Given the base and the area, find the height of each triangle.

   a) $b = 8$ cm
   $A = 36$ cm^2
   $h =$ _____

   b) $b = 62$ m
   $A = 186$ m^2
   $h =$ _____

   c) $b = 9$ mm
   $A = 63$ mm^2
   $h =$ _____

3. a) Draw a triangle with base 4 units and height 6 units.

   b) What is the area of the triangle?

   _____

   c) Draw a triangle with double the base and half the height of the first triangle.

   d) What is the area of the second

   triangle? _____

   e) What would you do to the first triangle to triple its area?

   _____

Stretch Your Thinking

A triangular plot of land has base 1 km and area 1 km^2.

What is the height of the plot? _____

Volume of a Triangular Prism

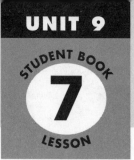

Quick Review

This triangular prism is 12 cm high.
Its triangular face has base 5 cm and height 6 cm.

We can use this formula for the volume of a triangular prism:

Volume = Base area × Height

Area of triangular face $= (b \times h) \div 2$
$= (5 \times 6) \div 2$
$= 30 \div 2$
$= 15$

The base area of the prism is 15 cm².

Volume of the prism = Base area × Height
$= 15 \times 12$
$= 180$

The volume of the prism is 180 cm³.

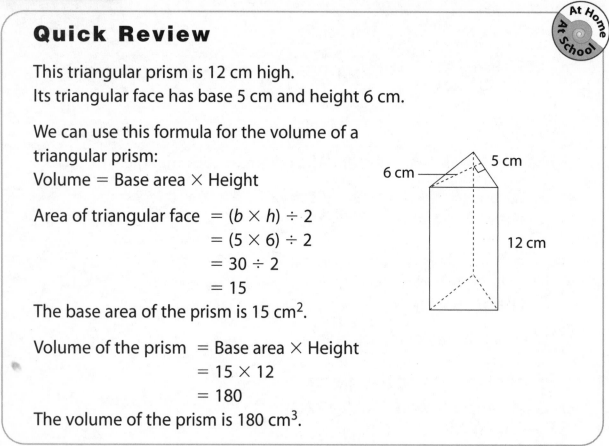

Try These •

1. Find the volume of each triangular prism.

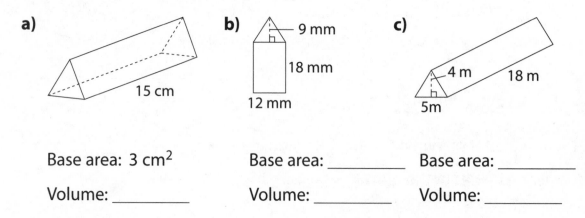

a)

15 cm

Base area: 3 cm²

Volume: _____

b)

9 mm
18 mm
12 mm

Base area: _____

Volume: _____

c)

4 m
18 m
5m

Base area: _____

Volume: _____

1. Find the volume of each triangular prism.

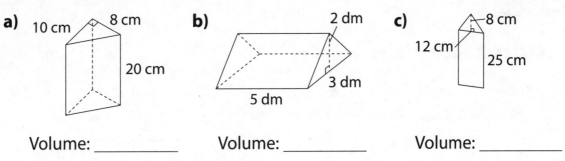

   a) 10 cm 8 cm 20 cm

   b) 2 dm 3 dm 5 dm

   c) 8 cm 12 cm 25 cm

   Volume: _____   Volume: _____   Volume: _____

2. **a)** What is the volume of this tent? _____

   b) How many campers do you think could sleep
   comfortably in the tent? Explain.

   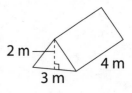

   2 m 3 m 4 m

   _____

   _____

3. A triangular prism has height 20 cm.
   Its triangular face has base 7 cm and height 10 cm.

   a) What is the volume of the prism? _____

   b) Suppose you triple the height of the prism.
   What happens to the volume? _____

   c) Suppose you triple the base of the triangular face.
   What happens to the volume? _____

   d) Suppose you triple the height of the triangular face.
   What happens to the volume? _____

   e) Suppose you triple all 3 dimensions. What happens to the volume?

   _____

Stretch Your Thinking . . . .

The volume of a triangular prism is 48 cm³.
What might its dimensions be?
Sketch the prism. Label its dimensions.

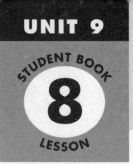

Surface Area of a Triangular Prism

Quick Review

At Home
At School

A triangular prism has 5 faces.
To find the surface area, find the area of each of the 5 faces and
then add the areas.

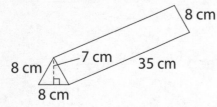

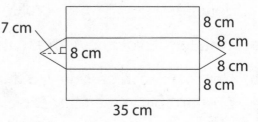

The area of each triangular face is: $(b \times h) \div 2 = (8 \times 7) \div 2 = 28$
The total area of the triangular faces is: 2×28 cm^2 = 56 cm^2

The total area of the 3 rectangular faces is:
$35 \times 8 + 35 \times 8 + 35 \times 8 = 280 + 280 + 280$
$= 840$

The total area of all the faces is: 56 cm^2 + 840 cm^2 = 896 cm^2
So, the surface area of the prism is 896 cm^2.

Try These

1. Calculate each surface area.

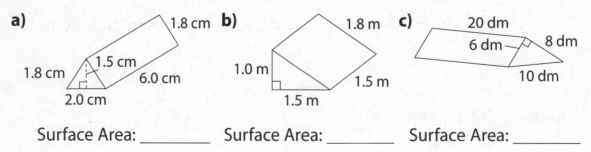

a)   b)   c)

Surface Area: _____   Surface Area: _____   Surface Area: _____

2. Order the surface areas of the prisms in question 1 from least to greatest.

_____

1. Find the surface area of each triangular prism.

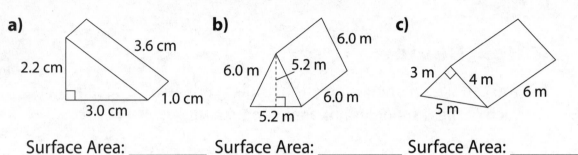

a) 3.6 cm, 2.2 cm, 1.0 cm, 3.0 cm

b) 6.0 m, 5.2 m, 6.0 m, 6.0 m, 5.2 m

c) 6.0 m, 3 m, 4 m, 5 m, 6 m

Surface Area: _____   Surface Area: _____   Surface Area: _____

2. A triangular prism has length 15 cm. Find the surface area of the prism if it has triangular faces with these dimensions.

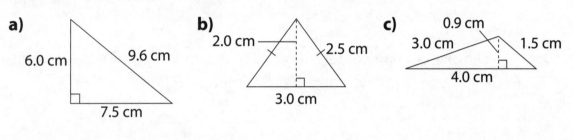

a) 6.0 cm, 9.6 cm, 7.5 cm

b) 2.0 cm, 2.5 cm, 3.0 cm

c) 0.9 cm, 3.0 cm, 1.5 cm, 4.0 cm

_____   _____   _____

3. **a)** Predict which of these prisms has the greater surface area. _____

   b) Calculate the surface area of each prism.

   Prism A: _____

   Prism B: _____

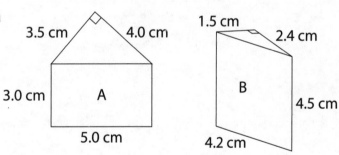

A: 3.5 cm, 4.0 cm, 3.0 cm, 5.0 cm

B: 1.5 cm, 2.4 cm, 4.5 cm, 4.2 cm

Stretch Your Thinking

Sketch the net for this prism. Label its dimensions.
Then find the surface area.

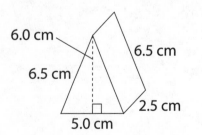

6.0 cm, 6.5 cm, 6.5 cm, 2.5 cm, 5.0 cm

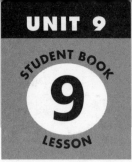

UNIT 9
9 Sketching Polygons
STUDENT BOOK LESSON

Quick Review

At Home At School

➤ You can sketch many different triangles with area 12 square units. Each of these triangles has area 12 square units.

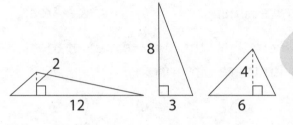

A triangle with area 12 square units has the same base and height as a rectangle with area 24 square units.

➤ You can sketch many different parallelograms with perimeter 16 units. Each of these parallelograms has perimeter 16 units.

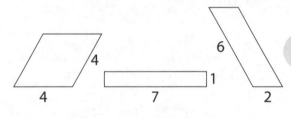

When the perimeter is 16 units, the sum of a shorter side and a longer side is 8 units.

Try These

1. Sketch 3 different parallelograms with perimeter 30 units.

2. Sketch 3 different parallelograms with area 30 square units.

146

1. Sketch 3 different triangles with area 20 square units.

2. Use a compass and a ruler.
   Construct 3 different triangles with perimeter 12 cm.

3. a) Sketch a rectangle with perimeter 26 units and area 36 square units.

   b) Sketch a triangle with area 6 square units.

Stretch Your Thinking . . . .

Sketch 4 different triangles with area 15 square units.

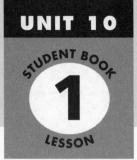
Representing Patterns

Quick Review

Here are some ways to represent a growing pattern.

➤ Model the pattern on a grid.

Frame 1 **Frame 2** **Frame 3** **Frame 4**

➤ Make a table.

Frame Number	Number of Squares in a Frame	Ordered Pair
1	5	(1, 5)
2	6	(2, 6)
3	7	(3, 7)
4	8	(4, 8)

➤ Draw a graph.

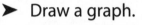

Number of Squares in a Growing Pattern

➤ Write a pattern rule.

The pattern rule for the number of squares in a frame is:

Start at 5. Add 1 each time.

Try These

1. a) Write the pattern rule for this growing pattern.

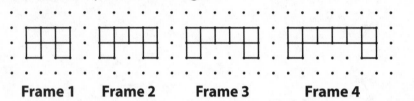

Frame 1   Frame 2   Frame 3   Frame 4   Frame 5

_____

b) How many dots are needed for Frame 10? _____

1. **a)** Write a pattern rule for the table.

    _____

    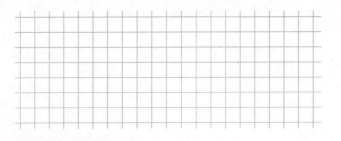

Frame Number	1	2	3	4	5
Number of Squares in a Frame	1	3	5	7	9

   b) Shade squares on the grid to model the pattern.

   c) Graph the pattern.

   d) How many squares are needed for Frame 10?

   _____

   e) Which frame has 29 squares?

   _____

   f) Which frame has 51 squares?

   _____

2. Draw a growing pattern to model the data in the table.

Frame Number	1	2	3	4
Number of Triangles in a Frame	1	2	4	8

Use the table in question 2.

How many triangles are in Frame 10? _____

Which frame has 8192 triangles? _____

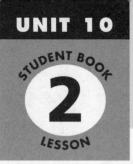
Relating Graphs and Input/Output Machines

Quick Review

➤ To draw a graph for this Input/Output machine: Make an Input/Output table.

Input ➡ × 2 ➡ − 1 Output

Then draw and label a coordinate graph.

Input	1	2	3	4
Output	1	3	5	7

Input/Output Pattern

(graph with points rising)

➤ To draw an Input/Output machine for the graph to the left:

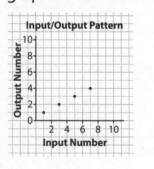

Input/Output Pattern

Make a table.

Input	1	3	5	7
Output	1	2	3	4

Then draw and label an Input/Output machine.

Input ➡ + 1 ➡ ÷ 2 Output

Try These

1. a) Make a table of input and output numbers for the graph below.

   b) Write the numbers and operations in the Input/Output machine.

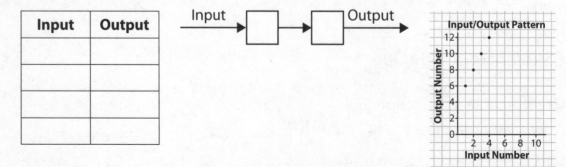

Input	Output

Input ➡ ☐ ➡ ☐ Output

Input/Output Pattern

150

1. For each graph, make a table for the input and output numbers.
   Write the numbers and operations in the Input/Output machine.

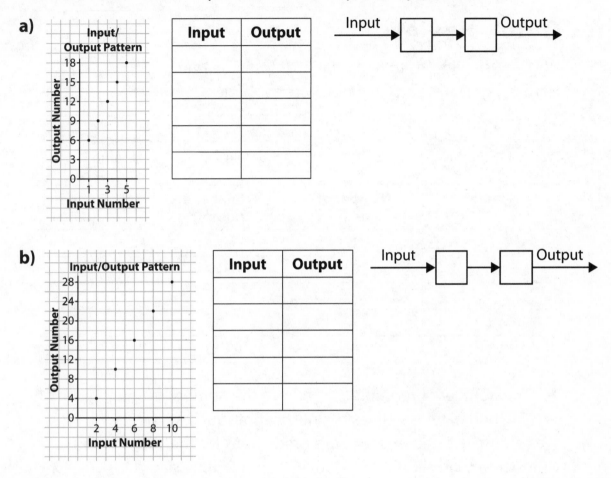

a)

Input/Output Pattern

Input	Output

b)

Input/Output Pattern

Input	Output

Stretch Your Thinking

The graph shows how much water is lost by a dripping faucet. Make a table to display the data. Draw an Input/Output machine that will produce the graph.

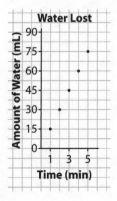

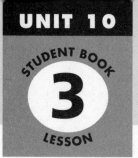
Patterns in Geometry

Quick Review

We can use patterns to find relationships in geometry.
Here is a growing pattern made with toothpicks.

Frame 1   Frame 2   Frame 3   Frame 4   Frame 5

Frame	Number of Squares	Number of Toothpicks	Perimeter (units)
1	1	4	4
2	2	7	6
3	3	10	8
4	4	13	10
5	5	16	12

➤ The number of toothpicks is 3 times the number of squares plus 1.
➤ The perimeter is 2 times the number of squares plus 2.
We can use the patterns to make predictions for the 10th frame:
Number of toothpicks = (3 × 10) + 1   Perimeter = (2 × 10) + 2
= 31   = 22 units

Try These

1. Here is a growing pattern.

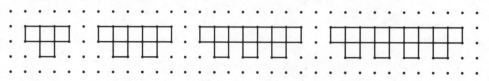

How is the number of squares related to the perimeter?

1. **a)** Here is a growing pattern. Draw the next frame.

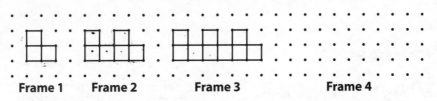

      Frame 1   **Frame 2**   **Frame 3**   **Frame 4**

    b) Complete the table for 5 frames. Then graph the data in the table.

Frame Number	Perimeter (units)	Ordered Pair
1	8	3 : 8
2		
3		
4		
5		

squares to perimeter

    c) What is the perimeter of the figure in the 10th frame? _____

    d) Which frame has a perimeter of 104 units? _____

2. Describe the arrangement of circles in the 10th frame of this pattern.

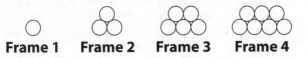

   Frame 1   **Frame 2**   **Frame 3**   **Frame 4**

_____

Stretch Your Thinking

 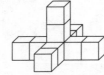

Frame 1   **Frame 2**   **Frame 3**

How many cubes are in the 10th frame? _____

Which frame contains 151 cubes? _____

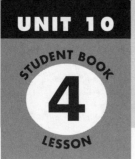

Relating Distance, Average Speed, and Time

Quick Review

Mitra rode her bike 8 km each hour. The table shows how far she rode in different times.

➤ We can display these data on a continuous line graph.

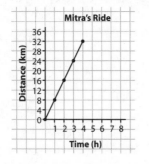

Time (h)	Distance (km)
0	0
1	8
2	16
3	24
4	32

➤ An Input/Output machine with × 8 will produce the numbers in the table.

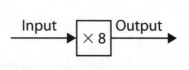

Mitra rides her bike at an average speed of 8 km/h.
Distance = Average speed × Time

Try These

1. For the table:

   a) Draw a continuous line graph.

   b) Draw an Input/ Output machine.

   c) Find the average speed.

   _____

Time (min)	Distance (m)
0	0
1	20
2	40
3	60
4	80
5	100

1. Basil took his boat out for a ride.
   He travelled an average speed of 35 km/h.
   How long did it take Basil to travel a total of 175 km? _____

2. Trudy's snail crawls at an average speed of 7 cm/min.
   Complete the table up to 5 min.
   Then draw a continuous graph to display the data.

Time (min)	Distance (m)
0	0
1	

3. The speed skater travelled 1200 m in 2 min.
   What was his average speed in kilometres per minute? _____

   Per second? _____

4. It took Bonnie 80 min to run 10 km.
   What was her average speed in kilometres per minute? _____

5. Sho walks at an average speed of 4 km/h.

   a) How far will Sho walk in 30 min? _____ In $1\frac{1}{2}$ h? _____

   In 3 h? _____

   b) Suppose Sho stops for lunch for 45 min.
   How long will it take him to travel 6 km? _____

Stretch Your Thinking . . . .

An airplane travels 4200 km in 6 h. How far will it travel in 4 h? _____

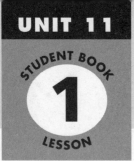
Describing Probabilities

Name _____

Quick Review

A probability tells us the likelihood of an event.

➤ When we find probabilities by performing an experiment, we find **experimental probabilities**.

$$\text{Experimental probability} = \frac{\text{Number of times an outcome occurs}}{\text{Number of times the experiment is conducted}}$$

➤ We can also write probabilities without doing experiments. These are called **theoretical probabilities**. When all the outcomes are equally likely,

$$\text{Theoretical probability} = \frac{\text{Number of favourable outcomes}}{\text{Number of possible outcomes}}$$

➤ Suppose you toss a coin 50 times. It lands on heads 27 times.

The experimental probability of the coin landing on heads is $\frac{27}{50}$.

The theoretical probability of the coin landing on heads is $\frac{25}{50}$ or $\frac{1}{2}$.

Try These

1. The students in Abner's class made this graph of their favourite fruits.

   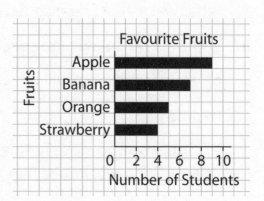

   a) How many students are in Abner's class? _____

   b) The students put the names of their fruit in a bag. Abner drew one name. Write a fraction to describe the probability that Abner would draw:

   apple _____   banana _____

   orange _____   a fruit _____   strawberry _____

1. **a)** Suppose you roll a number cube 30 times.
   Write a fraction to describe the theoretical probability of rolling:

   1: _____   4: _____   6: _____   7: _____

   an even number: _____   an odd number: _____

   b) Roll a number cube 30 times. Record your results
   in the tally chart. Write a fraction to describe
   the experimental probability of rolling:

Number	Tally
1	
2	
3	
4	
5	
6	

   1: _____   4: _____   5: _____

   an even number: _____

2. Suppose you put 15 jellybeans in a bag. A friend will draw 1 jellybean from it.
   Draw the jellybeans you would like to put in the bag for each situation.

   a) Red is more likely than green to be drawn, but less likely than blue.

   b) Yellow and orange are equally likely to be drawn.

Stretch Your Thinking . . . .

Each letter of the word MATHEMATICS is printed on a card.
The cards are put in a bag.
You draw one card from the bag.
What is the probability of drawing each letter?

M _____ A _____ T _____ H _____ E _____ I _____ C _____ S _____

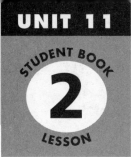
Probability and Percent

Quick Review

Georgette has 15 bottles of flavoured water in the fridge.
She has 7 bottles of lemon, 3 bottles of orange, and 5 bottles of raspberry.
Georgette takes a bottle without looking.
What is the probability that she takes a bottle of orange-flavoured water?

➤ Using words:
Only 3 of the bottles are orange.
So, taking orange is unlikely.

➤ Using a fraction:
The probability of taking orange is $\frac{3}{15}$, or $\frac{1}{5}$.

➤ Using a decimal:
The probability of taking orange is $\frac{1}{5} = \frac{2}{10}$, or 0.2.

➤ Using a percent:
The chance of taking orange is 0.2 or 20%.

Try These

1. Look at the spinner. Suppose you spin the pointer.
Use a fraction, a decimal, and a percent to describe the probability of each event.

a) The pointer will land on A.

_____

b) The pointer will land on B.

_____

c) The pointer will land on a number.

_____

d) The pointer will land on a letter.

_____

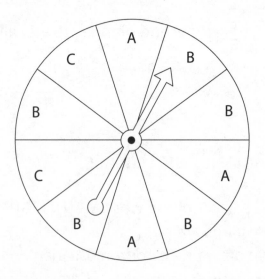

1. Gordon has 25 gum balls in a bag. He has 7 red, 5 green, 2 yellow, 4 orange, 1 black, and 6 purple gum balls.
   He reaches into the bag without looking and pulls out one gum ball.
   Write a fraction, a decimal, and a percent to describe the probability of Gordon picking each colour of gum ball.

   a) purple: _____

   b) black: _____

   c) pink: _____

   d) red or yellow: _____

2. Draw a spinner.
   Colour it so that the probability
   of spinning black is 30%, green is
   40%, purple is 10%, and red is 20%.

3. Vijay has a tub of 500 plastic jungle animals.
   Suppose he chooses an animal without looking.
   There is a 10% chance he will pick a giraffe.
   How many giraffes are in the tub? Show how you know.

   _____

   _____

Stretch Your Thinking . . . .

Design 2 different spinners, each with a 50% chance of spinning blue and a 50% chance of spinning red.

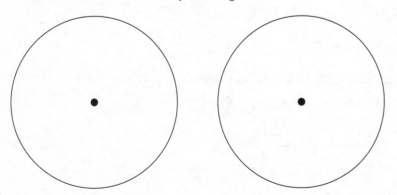

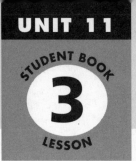

Tree Diagrams

Quick Review

When an event involves two or more actions, we can use a tree diagram to find and count all the possible outcomes.

In a computer game, the player must choose a path, a tool, and a disguise. You can draw a tree diagram to list all the possible combinations of a path, a tool, and a disguise.

Path	Tool	Disguise
mountain	rope	wizard
river	net	bear
desert		

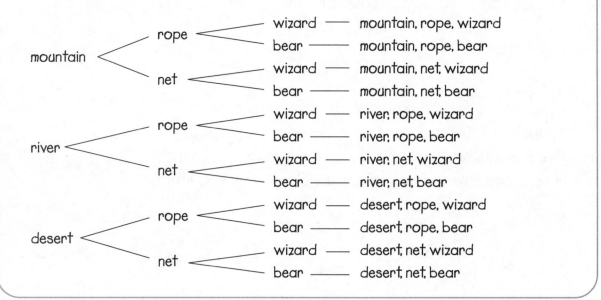

Try These

Use the tree diagram above.

1. How many combinations are possible? _____

2. Suppose you use a random selector button to choose a path, a tool, and a disguise. Find the probability of getting the following:

   a) river as your path: _____

   b) desert as your path and wizard as your disguise: _____

160

Use the following information to answer the questions.
The lunch choices of the day are a cheese or peanut butter sandwich
with either grapes, a banana, or an apple, and either milk or juice.

1. Make a tree diagram to show all the possible lunches.

2. How many different orders are possible? _____

3. What is the probability that an order will include each of the following?

   a) a peanut butter sandwich: _____   **b)** a banana and juice: _____

   c) a bologna sandwich: _____   **d)** fruit: _____

   e) a cheese sandwich, grapes, and milk: _____

Stretch Your Thinking

Suppose you spin both pointers
at the same time.
How many possible outcomes
are there? _____

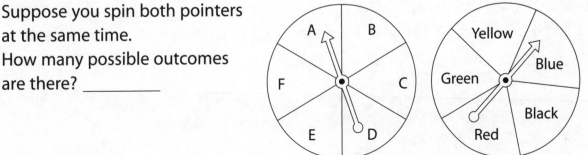

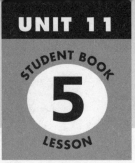
Conducting Experiments

Quick Review

Suppose you spin the pointers on these spinners.

What is the probability of getting A and 3?

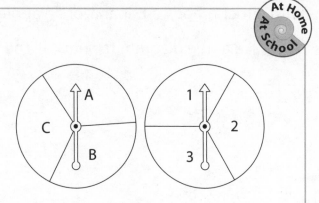

➤ To find the theoretical probability, Thom used a tree diagram.
There are 9 possible outcomes.
The theoretical probability of getting "A, 3" is $\frac{1}{9}$ or about 11%.

$$A \Big\langle \begin{array}{l} 1 - A, 1 \\ 2 - A, 2 \\ 3 - A, 3 \end{array}$$
$$B \Big\langle \begin{array}{l} 1 - B, 1 \\ 2 - B, 2 \\ 3 - B, 3 \end{array}$$
$$C \Big\langle \begin{array}{l} 1 - C, 1 \\ 2 - C, 2 \\ 3 - C, 3 \end{array}$$

➤ To find the experimental probability, Thom spun the pointers on the spinners 100 times.
"A, 3" came up 12 times.
The experimental probability of "A, 3" in 100 trials was $\frac{12}{100}$ or 12%.

Try These •

1. Suppose you put 20 green cubes and 30 yellow cubes in a bag.
Without looking, you draw a cube from the bag, record its colour, and replace it. You do this 100 times.
Write a fraction to describe the probability of drawing each colour of cube.

   a) green: _____   **b)** red: _____

2. Write each probability in question 1 as a percent.

   a) _____   **b)** _____

1. a) Find the theoretical probability
   of the pointer landing on each letter.

   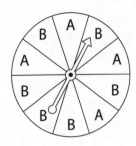

   A: _____   B: _____

   b) Use a paper clip to work the spinner.
      Spin 100 times. Record the results.

A	
B	

   c) Find the experimental probability of the pointer landing on each letter.

   A: _____   B: _____

   d) Suppose you combine the results with those of 10 classmates.
      How many times do you predict the pointer would land on
      A? _____   On B? _____

2. a) Play this game with a partner. You will need
      2 number cubes. Take turns to roll the cubes.
      Player 1 wins if 2 even numbers are rolled.
      Player 2 wins if 2 odd numbers are rolled.
      Play the game 25 times. Record the number
      of times each player wins.

Player 1	Player 2

   b) Is this a fair game? Explain.

   _____

   _____

In the game in question 2 above, what is the probability of rolling 1 even
number and 1 odd number? Explain.

_____

_____

_____

It's Amazing!

Tell a friend that you can look through number cubes to "see" the numbers on the other side.

Roll 5 number cubes that have been labelled as shown in the net.

After "pondering" for a few minutes, announce the sum of the numbers on the bottom of the cubes.

3	2	1
5	6	4

Here's how it works:

While you pretend to look through the cubes, mentally add up all the numbers on the top of the cubes.

Then, subtract the sum of the top numbers from 35.

The answer is the sum of the numbers on the bottom of the cubes.

Flip the cubes over, one by one, and add the numbers together as your friend stands in amazement.

Pencil Trail

Can you draw this figure without lifting your pencil? You can cross lines, but you cannot retrace any.

Think About It!

If there are 3 CDs and you take away 2, how many will you have?

you took 2 CDs.

Math at Home

Have you ever really wondered
How one million truly looks?
Could I eat one million candies
Or read one million books?

Would one million hockey cards
Fill the gap beneath my bed?
Could there be one million stringy hairs
Hanging from my head?

Do you think a large pile of sand
Could house one million ants?
Could there really be one million holes
Covering my pants?

Well, the other day, by surprise,
My teacher heard me say.
"I can't believe she really thinks
We learned one MILLION facts today!"

100-Chart Game Board

1	2	3	4	5	6	7	8	9	10
11	12	13	14	15	16	17	18	19	20
21	22	23	24	25	26	27	28	29	30
31	32	33	34	35	36	37	38	39	40
41	42	43	44	45	46	47	48	49	50
51	52	53	54	55	56	57	58	59	60
61	62	63	64	65	66	67	68	69	70
71	72	73	74	75	76	77	78	79	80
81	82	83	84	85	86	87	88	89	90
91	92	93	94	95	96	97	98	99	100

Risky Rules

You'll need:

➤ 3 sets of number cards, each labelled 0 to 9
➤ 20 counters
➤ a list of divisibility rules (below)

The object of the game is to be the first player to get 10 counters.

Before beginning, shuffle the cards, place them face down, and have each player take 2 counters.

On your turn:

➤ Draw 6 cards from the deck. Place them face down in a row to make a 6-digit number. No peeking!

➤ Draw another card. The number on the card represents your divisor.

➤ Turn over the 6 cards. If the 6-digit number can be divided by your divisor, with no remainder, take 2 counters. If not, give 1 counter to your opponent.

Take turns until one player has 10 counters. If one player loses all his or her counters, start the game again.

Divisibility Rules

A whole number is divisible by:

2 if the number is even

3 if the sum of the digits is divisible by 3

4 if the number represented by the tens and ones digits is divisible by 4

5 if the ones digit is 0 or 5

6 if the number is divisible by 2 and by 3

8 if the number represented by the hundreds, tens, and ones digits is divisible by 8

9 if the sum of the digits is divisible by 9

10 if the ones digit is 0

Multiple Mambo

You'll need:
- 2 number cubes, each labelled 1 to 6
- 2 different colours of counters
- 100-chart game board (on page 7)

The object of the game is to be the first player to earn 12 points.

On your turn:
Use one colour of counter.

Roll both cubes and add the numbers together.

Place a counter on the sum on the 100 chart.

Now, put a counter on the next 6 multiples of the sum. For example, if the sum is 4, you would cover 4, 8, 12, 16, 20, 24, and 28.

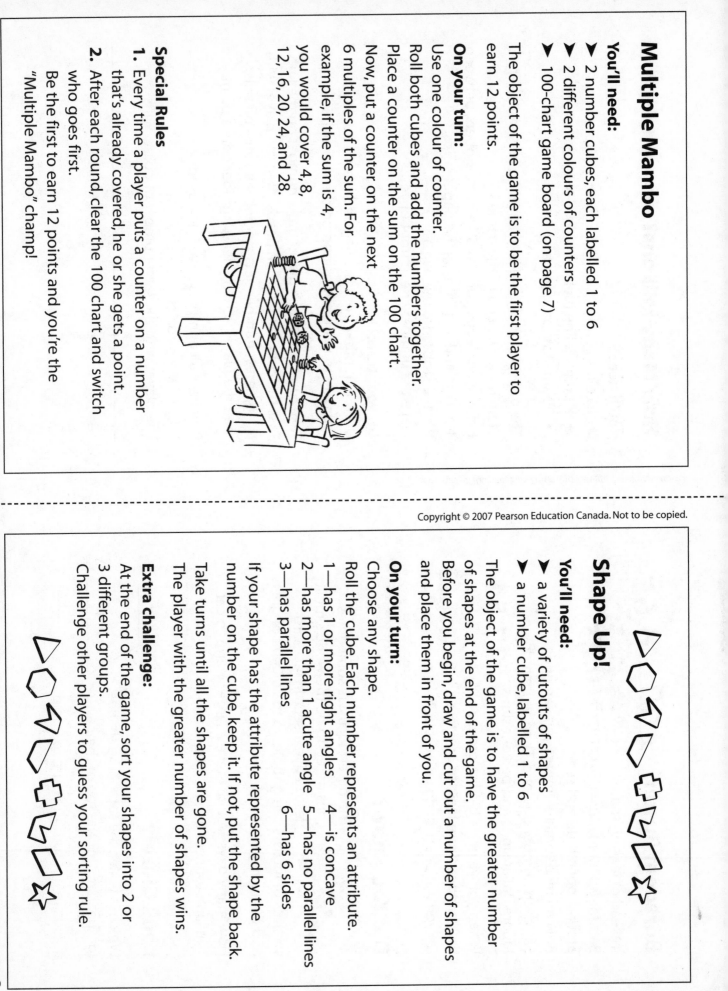

Special Rules
1. Every time a player puts a counter on a number that's already covered, he or she gets a point.
2. After each round, clear the 100 chart and switch who goes first.

Be the first to earn 12 points and you're the "Multiple Mambo" champ!

Shape Up!

You'll need:
- a variety of cutouts of shapes
- a number cube, labelled 1 to 6

The object of the game is to have the greater number of shapes at the end of the game.

Before you begin, draw and cut out a number of shapes and place them in front of you.

On your turn:
Choose any shape.

Roll the cube. Each number represents an attribute.

1—has 1 or more right angles   4—is concave

2—has more than 1 acute angle   5—has no parallel lines

3—has parallel lines   6—has 6 sides

If your shape has the attribute represented by the number on the cube, keep it. If not, put the shape back.

Take turns until all the shapes are gone.

The player with the greater number of shapes wins.

Extra challenge:
At the end of the game, sort your shapes into 2 or 3 different groups.

Challenge other players to guess your sorting rule.

How Many Millions?

You'll need:

- ▶ a coin
- ▶ a number line (below)
- ▶ 20 small strips of paper
- ▶ a paper bag
- ▶ pencils

The object of the game is to have the least number of points at the end of the game.

Before you begin, print 20 different numbers, between 1 million and 3 million, on the paper strips.

Put the strips into the bag.

Place the number line in front of you.

On your turn:

Draw a number from the bag and read it out loud.

Estimate to mark its position on the number line.

Take turns until each player has a number on the line.

Toss the coin. If it lands on heads, then the player with the greatest number gets a point. If it lands on tails, then the player with the least number gets a point.

Play until all numbers have been used.

Tally up your points.

The player with the *least* number of points wins!

1 000 000	1 500 000	2 000 000	2 500 000	3 000 000

Boredom Buster

3.27 8.65 10.25

Instead of leaving that Saturday paper lying around, open it up and see how many decimal numbers you can find.

Say each number out loud. Then, write it down. Ignore dollar signs and percent signs.   27.54

When you've got a big list, order the numbers from least to greatest. Do you notice anything interesting?

> twenty-seven and fifty-four hundreths … about twenty-seven and one-half

Did You Know?

The desert locust is sometimes considered to be the world's most destructive insect. In fact, large swarms of locusts can gobble up to 20 000 t of grain and plants in just one day!

How many days would it take a large swarm to eat 1 million tonnes? 2 million tonnes?

Look Closely

Which is wider, the top of the shade for the "lamp" or the top of the base?

If you are not sure, measure to find out.

Did You Know?

Suppose it takes 120 drops of water to fill a teaspoon. Since 1 teaspoon equals 5 mL, how many drops of water does it take to fill 50 mL? 1 L?

Bedtime Blues

Do you ever feel that you have to go bed before most other kids?

Conduct your own survey to find out if it's true.

You'll need to:

▼ Think of a good survey question.

▼ Ask a large number of students the question.

▼ Record your data in a table or in a graph.

You may be surprised at what you find out!

Think About this:

How might your data change if you:

▼ surveyed only Kindergarten and Grade 1 students?

▼ conducted the survey the morning after a school concert that ended late and that a lot of students attended?

What else could affect your results?

Fold

Math at Home

I heard so many things today;
There's not enough time to tell.
Shapes can translate and tessellate,
But are their sides parallel?

Do the shapes slide along like this?
Do they transform this way or that?
Are the angles right or are they not?
Acute? Well, fancy that!

These ones seem to rotate,
And make a pattern that repeats.
Wow! Do I feel dizzy ...
I need to take a seat!

Simply so many ways
To describe this shirt I wore.
But, this I know for certain:
This pattern's not a bore!

Centimetre Grid

Wrap It Up

Seth has 2 gifts picked out for Elena, but has only one piece of wrapping paper.

Can he wrap either gift, assuming he covers it completely?

45 cm

38 cm

10 cm
12 cm

25 cm
20 cm

5 cm
10 cm

Hint: *Think about each gift as a rectangular prism. Then, think about its net.*

Bargain Shopper

50% OFF
ALL KIDS' EYEGLASSES

Ages 12 and under.
No coupon required.
See store for details.

Find flyers for local stores.

Look for different ways that savings are announced.

Some ads may say

"Save _____ percent" or "_____ percent off".

Which way is easier to think about?

If you were a store owner, which wording would you choose to advertise savings?

(Think about how it might influence your customers.)

Can you find something that would cost only $20 at the sale price? $10 at the sale price?

What's the least expensive item you can find?

Time to Redecorate

You'll need:

▸ a number cube, labelled 1 to 6
▸ 2 different coloured pencils or markers
▸ centimetre grid (on page 7)

Design your ideal bedroom on the grid.
Be sure to include everything: dressers, bed, desk,
night tables, shelves, hamper … and maybe even you!
When you're done, it's time to transform, translate,
and rotate!

To begin:

Choose a piece of furniture to "move" first and roll the
number cube.

Each number represents a different transformation.
Move the item as indicated by the roll.
Draw the item in its new position using a different colour.
If the transformed image does not fit on the grid, roll
again until the image does fit.

1—rotate 90°
2—translate left or right 4 and up or down 5
3—reflect (You choose the mirror line.)
4—rotate 180° and translate to any new spot
5—translate left or right 2 and up or down 3
6—You decide how to move it.

Keep choosing new pieces and rolling the cube until
everything has a new spot.
What do you think of the new arrangement?
Challenge a friend to figure out how to translate, rotate,
or reflect each item back to its original position.

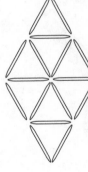

Triangle Tangle

Arrange 16 toothpicks as shown below.
Remove 4 toothpicks so that only 4 triangles remain.

Hint: The triangles don't
have to be congruent.

Did You Know?

Suppose a honeybee can flap its wings about
250 times in just 1 s.
Complete the table below to show how many times
it can flap its wings in 2 s, 3 s, and so on.
About how many times can a honeybee flap its wings
in 1 min?

"Wait up!"

Time (s)	1	2	3	4	5
Number of Flaps					

Time (s)	6	7	8	9	10
Number of Flaps					

Plot a Triangle

You'll need:
- ▶ 2 different coloured markers
- ▶ 2 number cubes, each labelled 1 to 6
- ▶ copies of the grid below

The object of the game is to be the first player to win three rounds.

To win a round, the area of your triangle must be smaller than the area of your opponent's triangle.

On your turn:
- ▶ Roll both number cubes. Use the numbers to create an "ordered pair." For example, if you roll 3 and 2, the ordered pair would be (3, 2) or (2, 3).
- ▶ Plot the point on the grid using one of the markers.

Take turns until each player has 3 different points plotted on the same grid.

Then, each player connects his or her coloured dots.

Compare the two triangles.

Estimate, then check, each area.

The player whose triangle has the smaller area wins the round.

Look Closely

Which is greater, the distance from A to B or the distance from B to C?

A

B

C

Believe it or not, they are both the same!

Fun with Words

Look carefully at each group of letters. Can you figure out what common Math term is "disguised" in each puzzle?

p l o t

"pair"allel lines

aller aller

graph

scatter plot graph

I Wonder …

Do you ever wonder why, on some days, it seems to take "forever" to get to the mall and at other times, the trip seems to go really quickly?

Conduct your own experiment to see what you can find out.

Here's how:

▶ On your way to the mall, set a timer or check a watch, and record the car's speed at one-minute intervals.

▶ Use a table like the one below to record the speed.

Time (min)	1	2	3	4	5	6	7	8	9	10
Speed (km/h)										

▶ On the way home, do the same thing.

▶ When you get home, look at your data and find the total number of minutes it took to travel each way. Calculate the mean speed the car was travelling for each part of the trip.

What did you find out?

Try the experiment on a few more trips to the mall to see how the data change each time!

So … is it all in your head, or does it actually take longer sometimes?

Fold

Math at Home

What's the chance that I can stay
Up late just for tonight.
Or skip my Math assignment
Without an argument or fight?

Is it really very likely
I won't have to eat my peas.
Or always use polite words
Like pardon me and please?

Are the chances very good
That my brother won't be mad
If I mess up all his stuff,
Then tell Mom that he was bad?

Although I'd like to risk it,
The odds aren't looking great.
Luck or probability …
I'd PROBABLY seal my fate!

Centimetre Grid

Is It Fair?

Chantal made a deal with her little brother, Daryl:

"If I spin the pointer on this spinner and land on a striped section, you have to clean my room. But, if you spin and land on a black section, I'll clean yours!"

Who's getting the better deal?

If you were Daryl, how would you change this spinner?

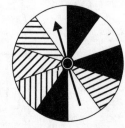

Did You Know?

A pip is the name for one of the spots on dice, playing cards, or dominoes.

How many pips are on a regular die?
How many are on 2? On 4? On 8? On 16?
Draw a table and see if you can *spot* a pattern.

Rectangle Rumble

You'll need:
▶ a pencil and paper
▶ 3 copies of a centimetre grid (on page 7)
▶ scissors
▶ a paper bag

The object of the game is to build the greater number of rectangles.

Before you begin, draw several rectangles of various sizes on the grids. Draw as many rectangles as you can on each grid. Draw one diagonal for each rectangle.

Cut out the rectangles. Then, cut along the diagonals so that each rectangle makes 2 triangles. Put the triangles into the bag.

On your turn:
▶ Take 2 triangles from the bag.
▶ Put them together to see if they make a rectangle. If so, keep both triangles.
▶ If not, choose one of the triangles. Calculate its area and keep that triangle. Put the other one back in the bag.

Special Rule:
If another player has a triangle that you need, you can take it instead of drawing from the bag.

Take turns until all the triangles are gone. The player with the greater number of rectangles is the winner!

Shape Puzzler

The shape below is made with Pattern Blocks. If the length of each side of the triangle equals 1 unit, what is the perimeter of the whole shape?

Extra challenge:
Trace the shapes of all of the Pattern Blocks and cut them apart.

Rearrange them to make a new shape with a smaller perimeter.

Now, try to make one with a greater perimeter.

Does the area ever change? Why or why not?

A Night Out

Suppose two friends go out for dinner.
They are seated at a square table.
Unexpectedly, 4 friends join them.
They quickly pull 2 square tables together.

But wait! Suppose 4 more friends
join the group and they add
2 more tables.

Friends keep arriving in groups
of 4. What might the arrangement
of tables look like if there were
12 extra friends? 16 extra friends?
24 extra friends?

Hint: *The pattern keeps "growing."*

Can you arrange the same number of tables in a
different way so that the same number of friends
can sit down?

How Old?

The age of a father and son add up to 66.
The digits in the father's age are the
digits in the son's age reversed.
How old could they be?

Hint: *There are 3 possible answers.*

What's for Lunch?

Rosie arrives at summer camp for
2 weeks.
She studies the lunch menu carefully and decides that
if she chooses a variety of items each day, she'll be able
to have a different lunch combo every day she's there.
Is she right?

Choice A	Choice B	Choice C
• Bagel	• Ham	• Cheese
• Roll	• Roast Beef	• Lettuce
• Pita Bread		

Hint: *Drawing a tree diagram will help you out here!*

Roman Numeral Challenge

Without lifting your pencil, draw one continuous line
to turn the Roman numeral IX into 6.

IX

Add the letter, S.